To
Alissa —

K.C.

Small talks on big questions

A historical companion to the children's catechism

Small talks on big questions

Illustrated by Caffy Whitney

by Selah Helms and Susan Thompson

joshua
press

Dundas, Ontario

Joshua Press Inc.,
Dundas, Ontario, Canada
fax 905.627.8451
www.joshuapress.com

Editorial director: Michael A.G. Haykin
Creative/production manager: Janice Van Eck

© Illustrations by Caffy Whitney
© Cover design by Janice Van Eck

Canadian Cataloguing in Publication Data

Helms, Selah, 1960–
    Small talks on big questions: a historical companion to the children's catechism

Companion volume to: A catechism for boys and girls.
Includes bibliographical references.

ISBN 1-894400-02-X (vol. 1)

1. Catechisms, English. 2. Bible stories, English. 3. Church history —
Juvenile literature. I. Thompson, Susan, 1961–   . II. Whitney, Caffy.
III. Title

BT1031.2.H44 1999   238   C99-931356-8

To my husband Doug,
who has faithfully taught our family that Christian doctrine is
more than theory—it changes our lives
—Selah

To Arch and Jackie Thompson,
whose encouragement has always been an inspiration
—Susan

Contents

Foreword by Jonathan Gerstner 11
Acknowledgements 13
Introduction 15

Unit I: God

God the glorious Creator

    "Behold, my creation" 26

    The starry messenger 29

Glorifying God

    Only a voice in the wilderness 34

    The true story of a blessed broken leg 38

One God, three persons

    The threefold comfort 44

    God's little champion 48

God's attributes

    The God who sees all 52

    The shepherd boy's amazing find 55

God revealed in Scripture

    Gift amongst the rubble 60

    The professor, the washerwomen and the preacher 64

Unit 2: The Fall

Eternal human souls

    A thief in paradise 72

    Merely the flames of men 76

The Fall of man

    "Where are you, Adam?" 82

    David Brainerd and his catechized Indians 86

Disbelieving God

The seed of rebellion 92

One man's crusade against disbelief 96

Inherited sinful nature

Like father, like son 102

The pear tree incident 105

Unit 3: Atonement

Regeneration

Former Christian "Enemy Number One" 112

No method will do 116

The covenant of grace

One step back, three steps forward 122

The monk who couldn't measure up 126

Christ's atonement

The King who died for one, and all 132

Three florins or one perfect life for your sins? 136

Justification and sanctification

The woman who was forgiven much 142

God's amazing grace 146

Christ obeyed and suffered

The cup of Christ's suffering 152

Life from death 156

Unit 4: Our response to the Gospel

Repentance and belief

The earthquake and the jailer's broken heart 164

"Look unto me" 168

The Holy Spirit

The opened heart 174

The man who tried to save Evans Mills 178

Those before the coming of Christ

The greatest day 184
The Maccabees: Defenders of God's altar 188

Jesus is Prophet, Priest, King

If Christ is for us, who can be against us? 194
King over all kings 198

Endnotes 203
Bibliography 205

Foreword

At the turn of the twenty-first century, we are facing an unprecedented need for literature to help the children of believers come to saving faith and to help those who know the Lord to grow to spiritual and theological maturity. Godly parents are crying out for aids to help them in this divinely ordained task. My parents both recently have gone to be with the Lord. The most precious blessing they gave to me and my sisters was a home in which God's presence was keenly felt, and in which Christian doctrine was daily table conversation. My father, as a professor and church leader, and my mother, as an author, would find ways to make the truths of Scripture and church history come alive, and would question us to make sure that we understood the truths being taught. Visitors often would remark on the way profound truths of the Word were discussed by even the little children. How often I wished that a tool would be available to help all believing parents create this sort of spiritual school of Christ around their dining room tables.

I am delighted to see this precious work address this area of great need. It combines biblical truth and illustrations from church history in a most creative way and includes questions to ensure the stories are not read without discussion. What a wonderful tool it is to help make family devotional times a lively blessing.

Please use this book with prayer. Even the best devotional and educational work cannot take out the hearts of stone with which all our children are born. Only the Spirit of God can bring true conversion and the saving knowledge of Christ to those of any age. The Spirit does make use of means, and lively discussions of his Word and his acts in history are wonderful means of reaching children and adults alike. Let these excellent studies and questions be the beginning not the end of your family devotional time. Don't rest until you know where your children are spiritually. May this excellent guide for family devotions lead on to personal individual spiritual discussions with each of your children and to the conversion of many of the children set apart for him in believing homes. Someday they too will take down their well-worn copy of *Small talks on big questions* and share it with their children.

Dr. Jonathan Gerstner
Professor of Systematic Theology
Knox Theological Seminary
Ft. Lauderdale, Florida

Acknowledgements

The authors wish to thank, first of all, our Lord Jesus Christ for involving us in the spread of his kingdom on earth, and for giving us truth so worthy of being spread. What a privilege!

Second, we wish to thank our families for their support in making this book a reality—by encouraging us, babysitting, and being willing to be independent during the time we spent on the book. We also thank our friends for reading the early drafts to their children and giving us feedback.

Third, we wish to acknowledge certain "trailblazers" who showed us the importance of doctrine and its practicality for a growing Christian's life: J.I. Packer, for his gentle yet powerful way of teaching truth, Jonathan Edwards, for the impact his Godward thinking had on his own family life for generations, Elizabeth Prentiss, because her tremendous knowledge of God translated into a very practical and active love for others, and C.S. Lewis, who had such a winsome way of capturing children's hearts with deep truth.

May our book in some small measure reflect our reverence for God's truth and our appreciation for the godly influence others have had in our lives!

Introduction

Why teach children doctrine?

*It is the authors' hope that this catechism companion will prove a
powerful tool with which parents can effectively educate their
children in the fundamentals of Christian doctrine.*

Christian doctrine is a statement of what the Bible teaches Christians to
believe about God and how we can know him. Orthodox Christian doctrine
is based entirely on Holy Scripture. From the time of the Reformation, such
doctrine frequently has been taught using some form of catechism, a method
of teaching by questions and answers.

However, teaching doctrine is out of vogue with many Christian parents
today. Instead, some choose to teach character as the basis of their children's
spiritual education. Others expect their children to comprehend Christian
doctrine strictly by reading Bible stories with them. Some choose an eclectic
approach—a little bit of this, a little bit of that—taking the best of several
different strands of often conflicting thought and/or approaches. The main
goal for some is simply to lead their child in the "sinner's prayer," believing
that to be the main hurdle of their child's spiritual experience. Others, wanting their teaching to be practical, purposefully avoid doctrine.

However, it is important to realize that everyone has a doctrine—a way of
understanding what the Bible teaches. Everyone who teaches children therefore provides them with some type of doctrine based on the perspective and
value judgments he or she brings to life. Thus, we must ensure that the doctrine
we teach is sound. All Christian parents want to teach their children biblically.
But "biblical" has come to mean a lot of different things to different people.
Good, orthodox doctrine arises from a proper understanding of Scripture.
Good doctrine provides a grid for being able to plot an understanding of family, daily life, science, history, friendship, emotions, beauty, work and worship.

Our goal is to equip both parents and children with a robust enough theology to answer the hard questions of life. Good doctrine will direct our thoughts to the right questions: Who is God? What does he require of me? How can I know him? How can I please him? Instead, our "felt needs" society directs us to ask how God can solve the little problems of our lives. Our human focus tends to be on how God can fit into our life plans rather than how we fit into his plan. A poor grasp of doctrine, or a wrong doctrine that concentrates on such secondary issues of life, can leave a vacuum in our children's hearts and make them easy prey for any "religious" group that offers them more than they think they are getting. With the question, "why did God make me?" and the answer, "for his own glory, that I might love and obey him in all I do," our children can confront all the secondary challenges of life with confidence, peace and joy. They have the big answer!

Fuzzy doctrine is a natural by-product of a fast-paced society in which most of us tend to be "doers" rather than "thinkers." It is easier. However, those in Christian work often find that, without good reasons for doing so, the people they minister to do not stick with the commitment required to truly take the Christian path. Why? Doing without thinking leads to a flaccid Christianity that struggles to answer the hard questions of life. As Sinclair Ferguson states in *Know Your Christian Life*, the best "thinkers" have historically been the best "doers." The best preachers, martyrs, missionaries and Christian civic leaders have been those who have grappled with the most challenging biblical teachings.[1] Indeed, the people who have most influenced *us* personally with respect to the gospel are serious students of Bible doctrine, even if they do not consider themselves as such. They are seeking to conform their minds to the Bible's teachings, rather than leading self-serving, busy lives that lack depth.

By-products of good doctrine are righteousness and Christian character. Christian character, as the sole focus and foundation of one's theology, results in nothing but morality. Simultaneously, an absence of strong doctrine naturally leads to looseness in Christian living. (The twentieth-century American church is a showcase for this point.) But teaching that stresses God's holiness and man's responsibility, along with God's gracious provision of Christ, will produce in individuals a Christian vitality evidenced by love, gratefulness, humility, duty and service.

Parents who were brought up with "the sinner's prayer" have a challenge on their hands. They may have come to believe that if our children pray that prayer, they are "safe" no matter what they do later in life. Yet a child may pray that prayer without a work of grace truly taking place in his or her heart. Salvation is by grace through faith, and not through a particular prayer. The sinner's prayer may be, and often is, an expression of faith, but it is not necessarily so. Rather, Scripture teaches that those who believe in Christ become his followers (Luke 9:23), and we must therefore disciple our children over the long haul, teaching them daily and hourly what it means to be followers of Jesus Christ. We must teach them that trust is more than intellectual assent, that those who love Christ will keep his commands (John 14:21), and that we must examine ourselves to see for sure whether our faith is genuine. Leading a child to examine his heart requires time, patience, commitment and understanding of doctrine, but will be worth far more eternally than giving him or her the false security of a prayer prayed on the surface of the heart.

We have great confidence in the ability of our children to profit from more than a "Bible stories" curriculum, and to absorb doctrinal truths from Scripture that will reveal the character of God in a personal way, explain God's provision for us from justification through glorification, and uncover the riches of a salvation that permeates all areas of life.

■　■　■

How to use this book

This book is designed to make the discussion and teaching of doctrine pleasant and insightful to children from age 8 and up. Many parents and teachers use a catechism in their instruction of children, yet it can too easily become just an exercise in memorization. The stories and questions in this book will foster open discussion and careful thinking about the ramifications of Bible truths, and the exciting episodes in the lives of real Christians will bring out how these doctrines have shaped history.

The catechism questions (referred to as "questions to learn") are grouped into doctrinal points, with a Bible story and a story from subsequent Church history to illustrate each section. We suggest that both before and after reading each story in a section, you go over the catechism questions for that section and encourage the children to memorize them. Then tie in the doctrinal concepts with the story events and the Scripture references. We include discussion questions at the end of each story to help accomplish this. Younger children might only learn the catechism questions and enjoy the stories. However, the discussion questions will help older children think through the abstract concepts. Lead the children to see that Bible truths are not separate from our daily lives; they lead us to life! Help them to see that knowing these truths will allow them to know the Lord Jesus Christ himself, and how to rightly worship and please him.

The catechism that the stories illustrate is taken from *A catechism for boys and girls*, published in the past by Reformation Today Trust and now by Joshua Press. This children's catechism is an excellent introduction to the *Westminster Shorter Catechism* and other evangelical Protestant catechisms.

■ ■ ■

Bible stories

The Bible stories that we selected to illustrate the catechism's doctrinal truths are imaginatively presented. To some stories we have added dialogue and/or detail that the Scriptures do not give, but in all cases we have sought to retain the accuracy of what the Scriptures do give. The goal is to draw children's imaginations into the biblical accounts, helping them to see the Bible characters as real people in history who were genuinely impacted by doctrinal truths. For those who wish to refer back to the scriptural accounts, our sources are cited at the end of each story. Note that italicized sentences within the stories are direct quotes from the NIV.

■ ■ ■

Church history

We have made no attempt in this book to comprehensively present Church history. Rather, we simply highlight persons and events that give evidence of

God's sovereignty and the truth of Bible doctrine. Therefore, our primary criterion for choosing the historic stories was their applicability to the biblical truths inherent in the catechism questions. Still, we believe we were able to touch on the most important periods of Church history, including the period during which the Roman Catholic Church was the dominant church, as well as the critical years leading up to and during the sixteenth-century Protestant Reformation.

In choosing between one or more events to illustrate a particular catechism concept, we considered the ages and probable life challenges of our readers. For this reason we tried to minimize the violence. However, Christian history does contain shockingly violent episodes, and we could not disregard the poignant and fitting testimonies of some of the best-known martyrs of the faith.

In addition, wherever possible we illustrated a doctrinal point with a story of someone championing that truth, rather than failing to live it out. However, in some sections we felt that a negative example was the best teaching tool.

Our Church history stories are based on historical facts, though we have added fictional detail (particularly in the dialogue) to make them suitable for elementary age children. None of these additions deviates significantly from any factual information available to us. Bibliographies for each story appear at the end of the book. Many of the stories are based primarily on the autobiographical writings of the central characters.

The following story, based on an account from the *Selected Shorter Writings of Benjamin B. Warfield*, illustrates how the catechism, taken to heart, can so enlarge a person's thinking as to stir him to godliness even in reactions he himself is unaware of.

■ ■ ■

No ordinary face in the crowd

The young soldier soberly straightened his uniform and prepared to step off the stagecoach at this, his first post since the Civil War had ended. Surely it would be a challenge for him to keep the peace in this town in the heart of the Confederacy, but he never suspected just how hard it might be.

Even before his foot touched the dirt, he heard gunfire, and saw the dust kick up where a bullet had missed its target. Moments later, a lanky gunslinger burst out of a storefront a few feet away, fleeing the shopkeeper's wild bullets. Most of the folk, milling boisterously through Main Street, dove for cover of whatever kind was available. Many tried to hide behind one another, far more willing for their neighbours to take a stray bullet than they were themselves.

"Take that, you rascal!" the shopkeeper snarled, her skirts flying up all around her. "Don't you ever show your lying, cheating face around here again, or I'll aim a lot closer next time." After she was satisfied that her victim was out of range, she went back into her store. The people in the streets emerged crossly, dusted themselves off, and quickly scurried for their homes.

It was late in the afternoon and getting toward the hour of day when the bitter, beaten Confederates had drunk enough to make it dangerous for everyone. The speculators and fortune-hunters, who now controlled all the town's businesses, didn't make it any better. They were charging so much for their goods that most regular folks did not have enough to eat.

The soldier, heading toward his new outpost across town, felt sorry for those in the crowd around him—their faces either pale and drawn, full of fear, or red and puffy, swollen with greed. Amidst this turmoil, he noticed a man approaching him from the opposite end of the street, calmly and purposefully threading his way around a group of quarrelling men on one side and an overturned barrel of grain on the other. Confidence, peace, and self-control were etched into this stranger's face. He seemed unruffled by the surrounding chaos and unafraid.

With much satisfaction, the soldier watched the man as they passed each other on the street. Unwilling to take his eyes from the serene stranger and return them to the fretful townspeople, the soldier turned to look back at the man's retreating figure. When he did, he found to his surprise that the stranger had also stopped in the street and was looking back at him.

Abruptly, the stranger turned on his heel, came back to the place where the soldier stood staring, and pointed his finger at the brass-buttoned uniform.

"What is the chief end of man?" the stranger demanded.

"To glorify God and enjoy him forever," came the young man's surprised but spontaneous reply.

"I suspected as much!" the stranger said, slapping his thigh. "I could tell you were a Shorter Catechism man by the look on your face."

"Why, I thought the same of you," the soldier laughed.

From the Bible:

So whether you eat or drink or whatever you do, do it all for the glory of God (1 Corinthians 10:31).

"Bring my sons from afar and my daughters from the ends of the earth—everyone who is called by my name, whom I created for my glory, whom I formed and made" (Isaiah 43:6b–7).

Talking it over:

1. *Why do you think the stranger asked the soldier the question?*

2. *To glorify something is to give it worship and honour, or to acknowledge its beauty. Do you think these two men glorified God in this situation? Why?*

3. *This young soldier had an unpleasant job to do (glorifying God in a tough situation). Think of something hard that you have to do. How can you give God worship and honour, or acknowledge his beauty in that situation?*

UNIT 1

GOD

God the glorious Creator

Questions to learn:

1. **Who made you?**
   God made me.

2. **What else did God make?**
   God made all things.

3. **Why did God make you and all things?**
   For his own glory.

■   ■   ■

God's glory is revealed through his creation and through his ongoing interaction with his creation. In this section, the story of Job and the events in the life of a scientist named Galileo Galilei show the glory that God displays in his world, and the praise it has elicited from mankind throughout the ages.

"Behold, my creation"

Job looked at his friends and sighed. A fine lot of comfort they'd been these past few weeks. His friends had only made his suffering worse, convinced as they were that he had done something to make God angry.

"How can you say you're innocent, Job?" Bildad said. "Don't you know you're a sinner? No one is righteous before God. You should quit claiming to be."

"You're a great help, Bildad," Job replied sarcastically. "I'm telling you I'm holding on to my righteousness. There's nothing hurting my conscience. I have left no sin unconfessed."

Job's friend Zophar frowned. He had already tried to tell Job that God only punishes wicked people. If Job were really innocent, he would still be healthy and rich.

Indeed, Job had once had ten beautiful children and had been considered the greatest man in the East. He had owned thousands of sheep, camels, donkeys and oxen, and everyone had respected him. Most importantly, he had always loved and obeyed God. Then God had allowed everything to be taken from him — his wealth, his children, even his health. He now sat, a little apart from his friends, scraping his diseased skin with a piece of broken bowl.

"Never has my heart been secretly enticed to worship the sun or the moon," Job declared to his friends. "I've been faithful to God and obeyed him. I've shared my bread with the poor. I've been true to my wife and children. I was kind to my servants and upheld right causes in court. Yet now God is against me for no reason, and I don't think it's right."

Job's friends eventually gave up trying to convince him and fell silent. As they all sat pondering Job's recent misery, a gust of wind caught their attention. A storm was beginning to brew off toward the west. The distant rumble slowly grew to a loud howl. Above them, they saw a black sky closing in. What they heard in the gathering winds and pelting rain caused them to fall face down. God was speaking.

"Who is this who questions my wisdom?" God's thunderous voice asked Job. "Were you there when I created the earth? Did you stretch a measuring line across it to mark off its borders? Who shut the waves of the sea behind doors and knit the clouds into its garment? Have you instructed the

morning or shown the sun where to rise?"

As God opened the secrets of the world to Job, Job listened fearfully. Who was he to question God's doings?

"Tell me if you really understand how big the earth is, Job. Have you seen where light lives, or have you cut channels through the earth for torrents of rain? Do you dispatch the lightning bolts, and do they come back and tell you where they are? Do you know when the mountain goats have their babies, and do you nourish the hungry raven?"

On and on God unfurled the wonders of his creation to Job, while more and more Job realized the wisdom and goodness of God. Finally, the storm subsided and Job was silent before God. Never had he fully understood God's ways until now! Everything in the creation belongs to God and he can do no wrong with it. He is holy and powerful and good. Thereafter, whenever Job did not understand something, God's creation was a magnificent reminder that God could still be trusted. God had shown Job his glory.

Taken from: Job 25–31; 38–39:1.

From the Bible:

[W]hat may be known about God is plain to [men], because God has made it plain to them. For since the creation of the world God's invisible qualities—his eternal power and divine nature—have been clearly seen, being understood from what has been made, so that men are without excuse (Romans 1:19–20).

Talking it over:

1. *To glorify means to praise, give honour or ascribe beauty. How did God use the creation of the world to glorify himself to Job?*

2. *If someone did not believe God created the earth and all the people, how do you think this belief would make them act?*

3. *How do you think a person would act who believes that God made him and all things?*

4. *How does God's creation of you bring glory to him?*

The starry messenger

The evening of January 8, 1610, was a clear and starry one in Padua, Italy, where Galileo Galilei taught mathematics at the leading university of that day. When the sun had finally dropped behind the horizon and taken the last rays of light along with it, Galileo quickly put aside his papers and started up the stairs to the top floor of his house.

When he arrived at the window that overlooked the garden, his breathing was rapid from anticipation. He was going to look upon parts of God's creation that had been hidden from man since the beginning of time. He would be the first to see them; God had chosen him!

Galileo sat down at the instrument that he had spent months designing and shaping, remaking and perfecting in his workshop downstairs. In fact, this was an upgraded model of the instrument that he had first fashioned last summer. This one, when he looked through it, brought distant objects 30 times closer and made them 1,000 times larger than they actually were. It would eventually be called a telescope.

Throughout the fall Galileo had observed the moon through one of his less powerful, earlier telescopes. He had seen that it was a very different object than the perfectly smooth and polished sphere that people since the time of Aristotle—almost 2,000 years before—had assumed it was. The real moon had craters and mountains much like earth.

Last night he had tried this newest telescope for the first time, and could hardly believe what his eyes had told him. Hoping to demonstrate that the planets actually orbited the sun rather than orbiting the earth, as history taught and the Church still firmly held, Galileo had studied Jupiter. Unexpectedly, however, near Jupiter Galileo saw something that men had never seen before—three small but very bright stars arranged in a straight line, two to the left of Jupiter and one to the right. Tonight he would check Jupiter again, and then possibly turn his lens to some new wonders.

Galileo found the bright planet in his sighting lens and noted again that without any magnification he saw none of the three nearby stars that he had seen the night before. Then he looked through the telescopic lens.

But wait. He must have focused on the wrong planet! He drew back and rechecked the sight, assuring himself that he had indeed found Jupiter. He looked into the telescope again, gasped, and then began to pace the room trying to imagine what this could mean.

Tonight, the three stars were all to the right of Jupiter! In the last 24 hours, could Jupiter somehow have changed directions in its orbit around the sun? Or, instead, did Jupiter speed up and overtake these stars in *their* orbits around the sun? Even Galileo did not yet guess that the whole universe does not revolve around our sun.

On the next night the sky in Venice was "covered with clouds in every direction," so Galileo could not look at Jupiter again until January 10. On that night, two of the stars were back on Jupiter's left, and the third star had disappeared entirely, apparently hidden behind the large planet.

Galileo sat back and sighed at the heavens. This could mean only one thing—these stars were actually moving around Jupiter, and not around either the sun *or* the earth. (Later, men realized that these bright orbs were moons.) Galileo was just beginning to discern that much of what people of his day believed about the universe was wrong: that the stars and the sun did not really revolve around the earth, making the earth the most important body in the sky. Man and the earth were much smaller in the universe than had previously been believed, and the scope of God's creation was considerably larger.

Galileo rushed to record and publish his observations and conclusions about the moon, the Jupiter "stars," and certain other aspects of our solar system in a small book called *The Starry Messenger*. Soon people all over Europe were making or buying telescopes and viewing these and other wonders of God's universe.

As Galileo studied the order and beauty he found through the telescope, he became one of the first to hypothesize that God holds his creation together in part through mathematical "laws" that keep the universe ticking like a well-designed clock. God's power and glory were clearly revealed in this precision instrument called the universe.

Through Galileo and other courageous scientists of his time, people began to understand, experience, and appreciate God's creation in ways they never could before. To be sure, many have not credited the wonders of the creation to God, but the most honest have felt the same humility that Galileo Galilei confessed to a friend in the midst of his early observations:

"I feel an infinite amazement, that is, I render infinite thanks to God, that

he has been pleased to make me alone the first observer of amazing things which have been obscured since the beginning of time." [2]

From the Bible:

The heavens declare the glory of God; the skies proclaim the work of his hands (Psalm 19:1).

And God said, "Let there be lights in the expanse of the sky to separate the day from the night, and let them serve as signs to mark seasons and days and years, and let them be lights in the expanse of the sky to give light on the earth." And it was so (Genesis 1:14–15).

Talking it over:

1. *What might Galileo have learned about God from his astronomical and other discoveries?*

2. *How did Galileo feel about God letting him make the discoveries he did? Do you think that his response glorified God? Why?*

3. *Name one of God's creations that you think glorifies him. Tell why.*

Glorifying God

Questions to learn:

4. How can you glorify God?

By loving him and doing what he commands.

5. Why ought you to glorify God?

Because he made me and takes care of me.

■ ■ ■

The right response to God's glory is one of wholehearted devotion and obedience. John the Baptist rejoiced to see Jesus growing in popularity, even though it meant his own ministry would wane. The sixteenth-century reformer Bernard Gilpin showed unwavering and loving obedience to God throughout difficult personal trials. In these ways, their lives brought glory to God.

Only a voice in the wilderness

The shore and shallow waters of the Jordan River outside of Bethany were teeming with repentant Judeans waiting their turn to confess their sins. John the Baptist, wearing his trademark camel's hair tunic and leather belt, stood in water up to his waist waiting for an old man to wade out to him.

"What sins do you confess, friend?" John asked the old man.

"I am a tax collector, and have often collected more money than I was entitled to, even from the poor. I…I kept much of it for myself," he admitted solemnly.

"And do you now repent of these sins and seek God's forgiveness?" John asked.

"Yes. I want to be right with God and to obey him."

John eased the old man backward, dipped him briefly under the water, and lifted him up again. John then turned to the crowd and addressed them in a loud voice, "I am baptizing you only with water to signify your repentance from your selfish, ungodly ways. But there is already one among you who you do not yet know, the sandals of whom I am not worthy to untie. *He will baptize you with the Holy Spirit and with fire.*" John said this because he knew that many of them mistakenly thought he himself might possibly be the Christ for whom all the Jews were waiting.

After the old man waded off, John glanced up to see who was next. As he did, he noticed a stranger coming toward them along the riverbank from the direction of Galilee.

John's heart leapt in his breast at the sight of him and beat furiously until the man arrived on the nearby shore. It was Jesus. John ran out of the water to meet him.

"You must baptize me, John," Jesus said.

"Oh, Lord, but I need to be baptized by you who are without sin!" John exclaimed. "*And do you come to me?*"

"*Let it be so now; it is proper for us to do this to fulfil all righteousness,*" Jesus assured him. So John consented and escorted Jesus down into the Jordan and baptized him. As Jesus emerged from the water, John saw heaven open up and the Holy Spirit descend and light upon Jesus like a dove. God had told John that he would know the Christ because he would see the dove descend and remain on him.

Then John heard a voice from heaven say, *"This is my Son, whom I love; with him I am well pleased."* John fell on the riverbank and worshipped Jesus, while the people crowded around them.

"This is the one I've been telling you about," John told the crowd. "He is the one about whom I said, *'He who comes after me has surpassed me because he was before me.'*" (By this he meant that Jesus' earthly ministry would begin after John's had, but that because Jesus is God he has always existed and therefore was before John.) "He is *the Lamb of God, who takes away the sin of the world! The reason I came baptizing with water was that he might be revealed to Israel.* He is the Son of God."

Two of John's followers listened most intently to this testimony. The next day, when they saw Jesus near the river where John was baptizing, they made their way through the warm sand and waiting crowd to reach him. When Jesus saw them, he turned and asked, *"What do you want?"*

"Teacher," they said, *"where are you staying?"*

"Come and you will see." So they went with Jesus to the house where he was staying and became his disciples.

Not long after this, John was baptizing at Aenon, near Salim, because the water there was deep and the people were eager to repent. He was disappointed when some of his followers interrupted him to settle an argument for them.

"Why are you disputing among yourselves at a time like this? Look at all those people waiting for our encouragement. Receive them!" John demanded.

"But Teacher," one of them said, "the one you baptized and said is the Lamb of God...well, he is baptizing just up the river, and more people are going to him than are coming to you! You must do something."

Again John felt his heart jump within his breast, and then pound with joy. "Ah," he thought, "he finally has begun his work! The kingdom of God is at hand, and my job is done."

To his jealous followers, John said gently, "I told you all along that I was sent only to prepare the way for him. Now that he has come, *he must become greater; I must become less.*

"Jesus is from above and is above all. He speaks the very words of God. The Father has placed all things into his hands. *Whoever believes in the Son has eternal life, but whoever rejects the Son will not see life*, for God will not forgive him. Now go. Join the others who have already left me to follow him and find life."

Taken from: Matthew 3:1–17; Mark 1:4–13; Luke 3:1–22; John 1:15,19–39; 3:22–36.

From the Bible:

After Jesus said this, he looked toward heaven and prayed…"I have brought you glory on earth by completing the work you gave me to do" (John 17:1a,4).

May the God who gives endurance and encouragement give you a spirit of unity among yourselves as you follow Christ Jesus, so that with one heart and mouth you may glorify the God and Father of our Lord Jesus Christ (Romans 15:5–6).

Talking it over:

1. *In the above story, what are the ways that John the Baptist glorified God?*

2. *When we believe and obey God with all our hearts, and tell others about him, how do the people around us respond to God? How did they respond when John the Baptist did these things? How does this response glorify God?*

3. *Why wasn't John the Baptist upset when his followers left him to follow Jesus?*

The true story of a blessed broken leg

November 23, 1558

My Dearest Sister Cecily:

I write to you not from the stockades, as you probably expected, but as a free man, and will soon be on my way back to you and all my dear parishioners in Houghton. The Lord has delivered me from my enemies in a most dramatic fashion! You must tell the story, as I can't bear for another hour to go by without my friends and family hearing all that God has done.

As you know, I was recently on my way to a martyr's death, to be tried for heresy in London before the infamous Bishop Bonner. He, of course, was, until a week ago, the puppet of Queen Mary, who had pledged herself an enemy of our "reformed" Christianity. She was determined that none would publicly acknowledge that the Bible is supreme over Church doctrine and that salvation from sin is through Christ alone.

Because I love you, though, I have tried faithfully to preach biblical truth to all of you whom the Lord has entrusted to my spiritual care. Of course, it was this preaching, along with my disagreement with many practices of the Catholic church to which Queen Mary was devoted, that got me into trouble with Bonner.

When I first got word that I was to be tried for "heresy," it frankly took my breath away. I knew that what Bonner termed heresy was in fact the truth given to us by the Lord in his Holy Scripture. Still, it stung to be publicly accused of the very thing I am so dedicated to fighting against—distortions and lies about the gospel of Jesus Christ.

I took this to my Father in prayer instantly, and he showed me that I might do more to reveal the deceptions of the Catholic church by publicly dying for the truth he has set out in Scripture, than by proclaiming it from a pulpit for the rest of a long life. And so I quickly came to welcome the idea of being beheaded or burned at the stake for my Lord Jesus. And if it would glorify God more for me to live, then he could and would accomplish that too, in whatever manner he chose. For this reason, I rejected the pleading of many friends to flee Houghton before Bonner's guards came for me.

I clung to the Lord's promise in Romans 8:28, which says, *"And we know that in all things God works for the good of those who love him, who have been called according to his purpose."* This I had preached in Houghton time and again. I knew that God had graced me with love for himself and that God had called me according to his purpose, first to know him, then to become rector there in Houghton, and finally to be accused of heresy during Queen Mary's persecution of the growing number of reformed believers. And I knew that the Lord fulfills his promises. Thus, I rested in the assurance that whatever happened to me in this crisis would be his working for my good and for the good of others who loved or would love him. I clung to this promise constantly, with thanksgiving and growing anticipation of what he would do.

I prayed it when the guards came to the church to arrest me on October 29. I prayed it during the long and difficult days of the journey to London when I was bound in ropes and fed too little. I prayed this when on the ninth day of our journey—not too far outside London—I fell from the wagon and broke my leg. And I prayed it when the guards cursed me after my accident, angry at the delay. Indeed, they overheard my prayers and ridiculed me for thinking that God had allowed me to break my leg for my own good. Yet they seemed to grow a bit frightened at this, and to wonder what this God I was so sure of might do next.

I was still clinging to this glorious promise when two other guards rode into our camp on November 21st to give us the amazing news that Queen Mary had died on November 17th. Most importantly, the new queen, Mary's sister Elizabeth, is sympathetic to reformed thinking and promptly upon inheriting the throne declared the martyrdom of reformed believers at an end. Shaken and surprised, my guards gently untied my ropes that morning, obviously reverent of what the Lord had done. I pray that they will be the first among those for whose good God performed these mighty acts on that road to London.

So you see, dear sister, my broken leg kept me from arriving in London until Queen Elizabeth ascended the throne! As soon as I am sufficiently healed I will return to you. But you must tell the story now so that the greatest good for the greatest number results from these events. To his Glory!

Your joyful brother,
Bernard Gilpin

For 26 more years the Lord did indeed use Bernard Gilpin to his glory. This beloved rector of Houghton went on many mission journeys throughout northern England to preach the truth of salvation by grace alone. He gave very generously to the poor until his death, opening his home to shelter boys in need, and establishing a foundation to build and operate a grammar school in Houghton.

From the Bible:

"This is to my Father's glory, that you bear much fruit, showing yourselves to be my disciples" (John 15:8).

Yet he did not waver through unbelief regarding the promise of God, but was strengthened in his faith and gave glory to God, being fully persuaded that God had power to do what he had promised (Romans 4:20–21).

Talking it over:

1. *Why did Bernard Gilpin go with Bishop Bonner's guards instead of fleeing so that they could not find him?*

2. *In what ways do you think God intervened in the events of the above story to take care of Bernard Gilpin? Why do you think God did these things?*

3. *Do you think Bernard Gilpin "bore fruit" that glorified God? (John 15:8) What was it?*

One God, three persons

Questions to learn:

6. Are there more gods than one?

There is only one God.

7. In how many persons does this one God exist?

In three persons.

8. Who are they?

The Father, the Son and the Holy Spirit.

■ ■ ■

Though a mystery, the Trinity is a doctrine central to the Christian faith because it explains how God has revealed himself to us. Jesus lovingly explained the Trinity to his disciples while still with them in body. Athanasius, an early church father who lived about 300 years after Jesus, defended the deity of Christ as well as the Trinity.

The threefold comfort

"Hosanna! Hosanna!" shouted the great crowd of Jewish festival-goers, as they poured down the path toward Jerusalem. *"Blessed is the King of Israel!"*

In the middle of the throng, the donkey carrying Jesus trod along over the palm branches that the people kept tossing down on the ground before it. Philip, walking a few steps behind the donkey, beamed, glad that the people finally seemed to recognize who Jesus was. This Passover promised to be a turning point in their ministry. Perhaps the Jews *would* make Jesus their king!

On the other hand, Jesus seemed reluctant to trust the people's change of heart. Or was it that he was unwilling to be their king? Philip couldn't quite put his finger on the problem, but something was amiss. Jesus seemed so sad. In fact, now that Philip thought of it, Jesus had lately talked quite a bit about leaving and dying. Philip could hardly bear the thought of being without Jesus. He hoped this glorious reception of his beloved master into Jerusalem would drive those dark thoughts from the mind of Jesus.

The next day several Greeks approached Philip and asked if they could see Jesus. But when Philip took them to him, Jesus did not say one word about God's earthly kingdom and his own leadership over it. He only talked about seeds that die, judgment, and his hour that had come. Jesus left the Greeks then, and seemed to withdraw from the crowds. That, too, was unusual. What could all this mean?

Jesus knew of Philip's bewilderment and turmoil. He knew, too, that the other disciples shared Philip's confusion, and he had compassion for them. He would do all he could to comfort them.

A few evenings later, as Jesus climbed the stairs to the upper room for the Passover feast with his disciples, he knew he was facing the end of his life on earth. He had not been deceived when the people had cheered and run before him as he had ridden into the city. Tomorrow the same people would all clamour for him to be crucified.

Gathering his disciples around him, Jesus was troubled in spirit and heavy-hearted. He had to prepare them for the crisis they were all about to face, but the disciples were unable to grasp what he was saying. When he warned them that one of them—one of the Twelve—would hand him over to those who wanted to kill him, they cried out.

"Is it I, Lord?" each asked him, having recently witnessed the triumphant moment when so many of their fellow Jews had shown Jesus their adoration and declared their allegiance. Jesus knew that the disciples would not want to believe that he was now going to be betrayed by one of those closest to him!

And this was not all. Jesus still had to explain that he was leaving them.

"Where are you going, Lord?" Peter asked. "And why can't we go with you?" Jesus saw the panic creep into the disciples' eyes as they pleaded with him not to leave them alone.

In the midst of their fearful questions, and his own impending anguish, Jesus reassured his friends with the teaching of the Trinity.

"*I am going to the Father,*" he answered. "*Anyone who has seen me has seen the Father....I and my Father are one.*" Then he told them not to be afraid when he left, because he wouldn't leave them all alone. He would be sending his Spirit back to them.

"*I will not leave you as orphans; I will come to you,*" Jesus promised. "*I will ask the Father, and he will give you another Counsellor to be with you forever—the Spirit of truth.*"

In their moment of great anxiety, Jesus revealed God's triune nature to calm the hearts of his bewildered friends. He knew that the strength of this truth would support them in the hardest hour of their lives when they would see him die on the cross, and would empower them to boldly face a future without his bodily presence.

Taken from: Matthew 26:17–30; Mark 14; John 12–14.

From the Bible:

May the grace of the Lord Jesus Christ, and the love of God, and the fellowship of the Holy Spirit be with you all (2 Corinthians 13:14).

"But the Counsellor, the Holy Spirit, whom the Father will send in my name, will teach you all things and will remind you of everything I have said to you" (John 14:26).

Talking it over:

1. *Do you think Jesus' teaching about the Trinity encouraged the disciples? Why or why not?*

2. *The doctrine of the Trinity is very important, even though it's hard to understand. God is one God, simultaneously existing in three persons—Father, Son and Holy Spirit. Some people have tried to compare this triune nature of God to a man being a father, a son and a husband all at the same time. But that comparison falls short because such a man is never three distinct persons, as God is. Others have compared the Trinity to the different physical forms of water—steam, ice and liquid. One reason this comparison fails is because the same bit of water cannot exist in all three forms at once. In fact, nothing we have on earth is a perfect picture of God's triune nature, because it is an attribute that only he has.*

   Some people, misunderstanding the Bible's teaching on the Trinity, have ended up believing that Jesus is not really God, just a created son of God. Others have believed that Jesus is the Father, and there is no distinction between the two. These two views are called "heresy"—a teaching that seriously distorts the truth of the Bible.

   Study the diagram below. Christians have used this diagram to show the truth of the Trinity without confusing the idea that God is both three and one. [3]

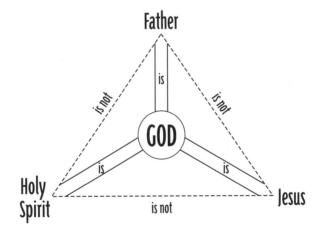

3. *From the story and above verses, what relationship did the disciples have with each of the three persons of the Godhead? (For a fuller treatment of these relationships, study all of John 14.)*

God's little champion

A tiny dark-skinned man leapt from behind a tree onto the Roman roadway. The Emperor Constantine unsuccessfully swerved the chariot to avoid him. Jumping boldly in front of the emperor's horses, the man grabbed a harness and held on grimly.

"Athanasius, let go!" the emperor ordered.

"No, I'll not let go until you grant me a hearing," the small man insisted quietly. "The Church is in danger, and you've got to help."

"You're a fanatic! You've lived too many years in the desert with the monks. We don't need an overzealous dwarf of a monk causing trouble in Alexandria."

"Jesus is God," Athanasius declared, undaunted. "You must support this truth in the churches. If you permit the Church to teach that Jesus is not God, the people will miss out on true salvation." With stubborn eyes, he tightened his grip on the harness.

"All right," the emperor sighed reluctantly, folding his arms. "You can appear before my court next week to plead your case."

God raised Athanasius up to defend this very important Bible teaching during a dangerous time for the Christian Church. For the previous 260 years, Christians had been burned, thrown to the lions and beheaded for worshipping Christ. But now there were new dangers—wealth and political power.

Since Constantine had come to rule over the Roman Empire, the persecution had stopped. After all, he was convinced that God had helped him to become emperor. So Constantine made Christianity the favoured religion of Rome, and he gave the churches and their leaders lots of money and land. Some of the Romans who had once persecuted the Christians now joined the Church so that they could become rich and important. Far too many people pretended to be Christians just to get the special favours.

These false converts didn't care very much about truth, so they did not mind much when a man named Arius started preaching that Jesus was created by God and therefore was not too different from other creatures, like animals and people. But Athanasius knew that this belief totally contradicted the Bible truth that Jesus is God. He also knew that if Jesus was *not* God, his

sacrifice of himself was of no consequence. If he were only a man, created like the rest of us, he would not have been able to keep from sinning, and only a sinless person can pay for the sins of others.

"Even if it's Athanasius against the whole world, I'll not give up this truth," the Alexandrian monk declared. Athanasius was firm in his belief that Christians must hold on to the fact that God is three fully divine persons and yet one being, and that Jesus is fully God.

Athanasius suffered greatly for his commitment to truth. His enemies sent soldiers to run him out of the city of Alexandria time and again. At one point, the desert monks hid him for several years while the frustrated authorities searched for him in vain. Although the "Black Dwarf" did not live to see truth triumph in this fight, he was confident that God would prevail against the heresy of Arius.

From the Bible:

In the beginning was the Word, and the Word was with God, and the Word was God. He was with God in the beginning. Through him all things were made; without him nothing was made that has been made....The Word became flesh and made his dwelling among us. We have seen his glory, the glory of the One and Only, who came from the Father, full of grace and truth (John 1:1–3,14).

Talking it over:

1. *Why was the time of Athanasius a dangerous time for the Church?*

2. *What was Arius teaching?*

3. *Why did Athanasius think it so important that Jesus is fully God?*

God's attributes

Questions to learn:

9. Who is God?

God is a Spirit, and has not a body like men.

10. Where is God?

God is everywhere.

11. Can you see God?

No. I cannot see God, but he always sees me.

12. Does God know all things?

Yes. Nothing can be hidden from God.

13. Can God do all things?

Yes. God can do all his holy will.

■ ■ ■

In the Bible story of Hagar, God reveals his omniscience, omnipotence and omnipresence to her in a loving and personal way. He has demonstrated these same qualities by preserving his Word throughout the centuries, as the modern-day story of the Dead Sea Scrolls relates.

The God who sees all

Hagar splashed some cool water over her flushed cheeks. The desert sun shone hottest in the afternoon, and the spring was cool and comforting. She believed that she had escaped from Abraham's tent without anyone noticing. Her mistress, Abraham's wife Sarai, had been especially harsh with her that morning, and when Hagar could bear it no longer, she had run away.

Hagar had made good time in her flight from Sarai. Surely no one would find her this far away. She glanced behind her. The road to Shur was little travelled and quiet. Yet she thought she heard someone calling her name.

"No, not here," she whispered, "not here." No one here knew her, and she was confident that Sarai's servants had not seen her take this path. Who would care anyway?

"*Hagar, servant of Sarai!*" The voice called again, closer.

This time she looked up the road. There, standing upstream, was a man whose appearance was unfamiliar to her.

"*Where have you come from,*" he asked, "*and where are you going?*"

Hagar did not even consider refusing to answer this commanding figure. Oddly, though, she was not afraid.

"I'm running from my mistress, who mistreats me," she answered. But she could not reply to the man's second question. She had no idea where she was going. Obviously, she was on her own now that she was away from Abraham and Sarai—the family that God had promised to protect and bless. No one saw or cared for her now. Surely even God would not watch over her now that she had run away from his chosen people.

The man smiled at her. "Hagar, go back to your mistress and obey her."

Hagar squinted up into the man's bright face. Just who was he and how did he know her name?

"I will bless you, Hagar, with many grandchildren and great-grandchildren. They will be too many to count."

Trembling, Hagar bowed down in worship. No one could make promises like that but the God of Abraham. The messenger told her even more. "You will soon bear a son," he promised. "You must name him Ishmael, which means 'God hears,' for the Lord has heard and noticed your misery."

"*You are the God who sees me,*" she said. "I thought I was hidden and

forgotten, but you saw me and you knew my misery. Nothing can be hidden from you."

Hagar did as the angel commanded her and went back to her mistress Sarai. A son was soon born to her and she named him Ishmael, as the angel of God had instructed. She named the spring where the angel had told her these things, "Well of the Living One who sees me," in honour of the God who she thought had forgotten her.

Taken from: Genesis 16.

From the Bible:

"O Lord, you have searched me and you know me. You know when I sit and when I rise; you perceive my thoughts from afar....Where can I go from your Spirit? Where can I flee from your presence? If I go up to the heavens, you are there; if I make my bed in the depths, you are there" (Psalm 139:1–2,7–8).

From heaven the Lord looks down and sees all mankind; from his dwelling-place he watches all who live on earth—he who forms the hearts of all, who considers everything they do (Psalm 33:13–15).

Talking it over:

1. *What did Hagar learn about God?*

2. *Look over catechism questions 9–13. How are each of those questions answered in the events of this story of Hagar?*

3. *Look up the words "omniscience," "omnipresence" and "omnipotence" in the dictionary. Can you tell which catechism questions these words go with?*

The shepherd boy's amazing find

"One of the goats is missing," the young Arab called to his companion. "I'm going to go look for him." He caught up his staff and canteen and headed back down the sandy road, following the path of the Jeep's tracks where the sand had been levelled and hardened.

"The goat has probably not kept to the same path," he mused. So he struck off down one of the steep valleys to look in the underbrush. High above, the sheer, stern cliffs watched him go. He felt awed by their silent gaze.

The Judean foothills west of the Dead Sea were full of old caves into which a stray goat might wander. But there were so many! Which should he look in? The boy walked rather aimlessly, farther and farther from his companion and the rest of the herd.

On an impulse, he picked up a piece of sandstone and threw it up into a cave in the side of the hill above him. Anything to break the intimidating silence. Unexpectedly, something shattered in the cave, convincing him by its echo that it was some sort of pottery.

"Antiques, perhaps," he said to himself. Very old Judean pottery was selling for a good price in the marketplace.

"Abdul, come!" he called as loudly as he could. "I think I found some antiques!"

Abdul joined him at the hillside cave. In the dim light they saw many old pottery jars that smelled of musty leather and tar. They tipped one over to examine its contents and found ancient leather scrolls wrapped in linen and covered with pitch.

"These could bring us a hundred pounds at the antique dealers' shop," Abdul speculated. "I wonder how many we can carry."

The two youths gathered some of the old parchments and set off for Bethlehem, but it took several weeks of bargaining before they found a buyer. The scrolls, which had portions of the Bible written on them, passed through the hands of several different dealers and scholars before anyone realized the significance of the discovery made by the Arab shepherd boys that day in 1947. When they were finally scrutinized by a well-known authority at John Hopkins University in the United States, the findings rocked the scholarly community and then the world.

Amazed scholars dated the scrolls at about 100 B.C., which was 1,000 years older than the earliest known Hebrew biblical manuscripts. Further trips to the cave and to other caves nearby uncovered hundreds of scrolls and scroll fragments. Genesis, Deuteronomy, Isaiah and the Psalms were found in almost the same form—except in Hebrew—as the form in which we have them today. Some consider the scrolls to be the most astonishing and important archeological discovery of modern times.

What did the findings prove? Many twentieth-century scholars have taught that the Bible—written so long ago—does not hold true accounts of historical events. These critics reasoned that the stories could not be trusted because of how much they must have changed as they were passed down through the centuries. But the Dead Sea Scrolls have helped to prove them wrong. Bible scholars saw how closely the scrolls matched the later manuscripts that were used for our current translations of the Bible. So they knew that the Bible stories have been accurately and carefully preserved throughout the hundreds of years since the events they describe.

The discovery of the scrolls also proved God's sovereignty in defending the truth of his Word. All through those hundreds of years while the scrolls were hidden, God knew they were there. God saw when the makers of the precious scrolls deposited them in the caves about 30 years before Jesus was born. God saw when, 30 years after Christ was resurrected, Roman soldiers burned the small community where the scrolls had been made. God saw when, years later, the ruins of this community were used as a hiding place for Jews rebelling against Roman rule. And God watched over the scrolls for 1,800 years after that, when nothing but wild animals visited the caves, and the manuscripts were forgotten by everyone but the desert. God preserved these ancient copies of his Word, and he determined—in his sovereignty and for his own purposes—that they would be found in our day to show the error of those who attack the accuracy of Holy Scripture.

From the Bible:

"Am I only a God nearby," declares the Lord, "and not a God far away? Can anyone hide in secret places so that I cannot see him?" declares the Lord. "Do not I fill heaven and earth?" declares the Lord (Jeremiah 23:23–24).

Nothing in all creation is hidden from God's sight (Hebrews 4:13a).

[H]e determined the times set for them and the exact places where they should live. God did this so that men would seek him and perhaps reach out for him and find him, though he is not far from each one of us (Acts 17:26b–27).

Talking it over:

1. *Did God know about the caves filled with Bible scrolls, even when no one else did?*

2. *Why do you think God allowed the scrolls to be hidden from men for so long?*

3. *Does the fact that God knows everything and sees everything comfort you, or scare you? Why?*

God revealed in Scripture

Questions to learn:

14. Where do you learn how to love and obey God?

In the Bible alone.

15. Who wrote the Bible?

Holy men who were taught by the Holy Spirit.

■   ■   ■

For a time in Israel's history, God's people lost his Word. Judah's high priest, Hilkiah, would have seen the effects of this loss on their hearts and behaviour. With the Scriptures again in hand, the Jews learned—as did the seventeenth-century English pastor and writer John Bunyan in the second story—that without knowledge of what the Bible teaches, we unwittingly violate God's commands and ignore his promises. Only with such knowledge can we ever hope to understand what it means to love and obey God.

Gift amongst the rubble

Tightly clutching the note he had just received, Hilkiah sped through the outer rooms of the temple to his chamber. He was Judah's high priest, and he dared to hope that this letter was another of young King Josiah's proclamations to cleanse the nation of all worship of false gods.

"How could these disobedient Jews think that a doll carved out of stone or wood, or even cast in gold, could work miracles for them or answer their prayers?" Hilkiah wondered, shaking his head in disgust and sadness. "And how could they actually bring themselves to worship Asherah poles, while they turn their backs on the living Almighty God who has real authority over all creation?"

But Hilkiah knew only too well why they did such things—because they had forgotten much of what God had commanded them. Centuries before, God had instructed their forefathers in how to lead righteous and productive lives that were pleasing to him. He had presented these commands to Moses, who had written them down and then read them to the Jewish people before they had crossed the Jordan River and entered the Promised Land that God had given them.

To Joshua, who actually led the people into the Promised Land, God had commanded further: *Be careful to obey all the law my servant Moses gave you; do not turn from it to the right or to the left, that you may be successful wherever you go. Do not let this Book of the Law depart from your mouth; meditate on it day and night, so that you may be careful to do everything written in it. Then you will be prosperous and successful.* The "Book of the Law" was the portion of the Bible that existed at that time.

"If only we had obeyed this command," Hilkiah sighed. Instead, the people had lost or disregarded the Book of the Law over and over throughout the generations. And in part because they did not know it to obey it, they repeatedly violated God's commands that were written in it, most especially his command not to worship any other gods. As far as Hilkiah knew, all copies of the Book of the Law were lost or hidden away. None had been seen during his lifetime.

"Lord, please give us your words again so that we will know how to please you," Hilkiah whispered in prayer as he ripped open the letter and

read the following order from King Josiah: "Hilkiah, now that we have purged Judah of high places, Asherah poles, carved idols and cast images, I'm sending you my men to help in purifying the temple of God. I know you will receive this news joyfully. Your faithful friend—Josiah."

With all his heart Hilkiah worked side by side with the king's men over the next few months to restore the temple of God. It had been looted and misused during the reigns of several recent kings of Judah whose riches had gone to building altars to false gods and paying the salaries of wicked men who called themselves priests of those gods.

One day Hilkiah was working alone in a secluded corner of the temple, removing debris from where a portion of the wall had fallen in. Thinking he saw a thin flap of some kind just beneath one of the stones balanced on the edge of the hole, he heaved the stone onto the pile of debris and gazed upon the object now exposed—a parchment scroll.

Trembling, Hilkiah picked up the scroll and gently unrolled the first few inches. There, at the very top, it read, "In the beginning God created the heavens and the earth."

He hugged the scroll to his chest and stood for a long moment with his eyes shut tight. "Oh Lord God, all-knowing, faithful and merciful, you have answered my prayer! Thank you for your provision."

Hilkiah could barely contain himself. He rushed to the king's secretary, Shaphan, who was overseeing the restoration of the temple. "*I have found the Book of the Law.* You must take it to the king immediately," Hilkiah urged him, handing him the scroll.

Shaphan did as Hilkiah asked, and read the book to King Josiah. After Josiah heard God's commands and realized how seriously he and his people had violated them, he tore his clothes and fell to the floor weeping. The king repented of these sins, and by reading the Book of the Law to his people, he led them into repentance as well. During King Josiah's reign, the people of Judah stored God's Word in their hearts and obeyed it, and God held back from them the punishment that he would soon bring against his chosen people because of their many centuries of disobedience. The Holy Spirit thereafter led the Lord's prophets to record this story in the books of Kings and Chronicles to ensure that future generations could learn of the importance of God's Word.

Taken from: 2 Kings 22–23; 2 Chronicles 34–35; Joshua 1:7b–8.

From the Bible:

Love the Lord your God with all your heart and with all your soul and with all your strength. These commandments that I give you today are to be upon your hearts. Impress them on your children. Talk about them when you sit at home and when you walk along the road, when you lie down and when you get up (Deuteronomy 6:5–7).

They are not just idle words for you—they are your life (Deuteronomy 32:47a).

And we have the word of the prophets made more certain, and you will do well to pay attention to it, as to a light shining in a dark place, until the day dawns and the morning star rises in your hearts. Above all, you must understand that no prophecy of Scripture came about by the prophet's own interpretation. For prophecy never had its origin in the will of man, but men spoke from God as they were carried along by the Holy Spirit (2 Peter 1:19–21).

Talking it over:

1. *Why was it so important for the people in the story to have God's commands written down where they could read them frequently?*

2. *When they had lost God's written commands, how did the Jewish people behave?*

3. *When Josiah had God's commands, how did he respond?*

4. *What do you think your life would be like without God's Word?*

The professor, the washerwomen and the preacher

Three hundred years ago, in a tiny English village north of London, God began to prick the conscience of a young man named John Bunyan. On this sunny summer afternoon, John had tired of the repair work he did to support his family, and had gone in search of something more exciting. Soon he came upon his friend Tom in the churchyard. Tom called himself a "professor," because he professed to be a Christian.

The two made their way to the belfry to ring the church bells, a favourite pastime of villagers who were putting off doing their work. While they took turns pulling the coarse, heavy ropes to coax the bells back and forth, Tom told John about the exciting stories he had read in his Bible. Tom talked so pleasantly about the Scriptures, in fact, that John soon spent all his evenings poring through the Old Testament for himself, reading about Moses and David and Daniel, and all the other brave and righteous men that God had used thousands of years before to accomplish his purposes.

Seeing that his own behaviour fell far short of these men of God, John began to imitate them in every way he could think of. He stopped cursing and swearing, and even left off bell ringing and got busy with his repair work. After a time, John had changed so much that the other villagers began to think him a very fine fellow. This opinion he shared.

One morning as John travelled to nearby Bedford to do some repairs, he fell into his newfound habit of musing about how pleased God must surely be with him. While in that state, he came upon several women talking about the Bible as they took a short rest from their work. He drew near, aiming perhaps to shed a little light on their understanding of that holy book.

"When Pastor preached last Sabbath from Paul's letter to Rome, I thought my own wretchedness would weigh my soul down to the grave. My righteous works are but dirt in his sight," related a stout, gray-haired woman, waving two grimy rough hands. The others smiled and nodded their agreement with this pronouncement.

Surprised by such a humble admission, John looked from one calm face

to the next, and was just about to set them all straight on the matter of personal righteousness, when a young woman said, "Thanks be to God for the mercy and grace he has shown us through the sacrifice of the Lord Jesus!" And with that, she whisked her skirts around her in glee. The other ladies clapped for joy and the one with dirty hands gave a hearty "Amen!"

John listened as they talked of Satan's many attacks on them, and their resulting discouragement. But then, each one eagerly took a turn telling how God had borne her up under these temptations and given her strength to believe.

John soon realized that he had no wisdom of his own to offer on these subjects. All the way home he pondered the women's conversation, and determined that he would go to hear for himself what the Bedford pastor had to say.

Returning from one of these Bedford services, John met up with his old friend Tom, who was bubbling over about a new group he had joined called the Ranters.

"Are these Ranters a holy group?" asked John.

"Why, to be sure, John. All the professors I know are turning to the teachings of the Ranters," Tom assured him.

"But the Ranters I know of have been accused of drunkenness, swearing and all manner of uncleanness," exclaimed John.

Tom laughed. "You are so straight and narrow, my friend. This new teaching reveals to us how we can do what we want and yet not sin."

"How's that?" asked John a little nervously.

"If we have the light of God in us, then doesn't it follow that whatever we do is really God's doing because he's in us?"

John considered this, then asked, " Does that mean you are always righteous, Tom?"

"To be sure, John. I do what I will, and trust that God's a leadin' me. Many a religion I have tasted, and only now have found the right."

"This teaching has an appeal to my senses," John confessed, worried.

"John, you are young yet! Do you think you will subdue your young passions? Live a life of freedom! Meet us at the barn north of town for the service tonight, and we'll help you along."

"I'll consider it Tom," John said as he walked away, thinking about how nice it would be to do whatever he wanted and not have to worry about whether he was displeasing God. But the idea scared him too, and he went home and got on his knees:

> *O Lord, I am a fool, and not able to know the truth from error; Lord leave me not to my own blindness, either to approve of, or condemn this doctrine; if it be of God, let me not despise it; if it be of the devil, let me not embrace it. Lord, I lay my soul, in this matter, only at thy foot, let me not be deceived, I humbly beseech thee.* [4]

Then John began to read his Bible—all of it. He read all afternoon, all evening while the Ranters were meeting, and throughout the night. He kept reading and meditating on God's words whenever he could for days and weeks.

God answered John's prayer and showed him that Tom was wrong. The Ranters were teaching and living in a way that the Scriptures condemned, and John soon understood that following the Ranters would be loving himself rather than loving God. The only way John could love and obey God was to know and follow God's teaching in the Bible. John Bunyan always remembered this lesson, and sought to shape his life wholly around the teaching of Scripture.

Later, God showed John that he had been given the gift of preaching the Word. John read in Scripture that he was to practice the gifts God had given him, and so he preached even when the authorities told him to stop in 1660. He refused to disobey God even when the authorities threatened to put him in jail unless he stopped preaching. And for 12 years he sat in prison, studying the Bible, trusting its truth, and writing books that would encourage countless others to love and obey God.

From the Bible:

> Do not add to what I command you and do not subtract from it, but keep the commands of the Lord your God that I give you (Deuteronomy 4:2).

> All Scripture is God-breathed and is useful for teaching, rebuking, correcting and training in righteousness (2 Timothy 3:16a).

Talking it over:

1. *Although John Bunyan wanted to please God, at first he didn't know how to. Why didn't he know how to please God? How and when did he learn how to?*

2. *When someone told John Bunyan how to act in order to please God, what did he do? What should you do if someone tells you to do something that they claim will please God?*

3. *Did God leave anything out of the Bible that we need to know in order to love and obey him? (See Deuteronomy 4:2.)*

UNIT 2

THE FALL

Eternal human souls

Questions to learn:

16. Who were our first parents?

Adam and Eve.

17. Of what were our first parents made?

God made the body of Adam out of the ground, and formed Eve from the body of Adam.

18. What did God give Adam and Eve besides bodies?

He gave them souls that could never die.

19. Have you a soul as well as a body?

Yes. I have a soul that can never die.

20. How do you know that you have a soul?

Because the Bible tells me so.

■　　■　　■

Incredibly, one of the robbers crucified with Jesus joined the crowd in taunting him. The other one, confronted by what he doubtless feared would be a dark and miserable eternity, asked Jesus to remember him and was surprised by joy when Jesus promised to take him to paradise. Polycarp, who lived only a century later, had full assurance of the life of his soul after death, and this enabled him to face persecution unafraid.

A thief in paradise

Up the hill outside of Jerusalem, the condemned man dragged a huge cross bar that cut a deep channel into the mud behind him. Near the top, he slipped and the lumber rolled off his shoulder, smashing into the heel of his left foot just as a soldier's whip lashed him across the neck and face.

The prisoner, the last of three to be crucified, somehow managed to crawl the last few yards to the summit of "the Skull," tugging the bar along beside him. "It has come to this!" he exclaimed to himself, over and over. "It's really happening. They are going to kill me." And with that thought, the panic rose in his heart like floodwaters and began to choke the breath from his lungs.

As he lay in the mud waiting to be tortured, the man watched the guards nail the first prisoner to the first cross bar. He saw the blows strike in succession, each followed a moment later by an agonizing scream of pain, and he imagined the sharp metal ripping through his own flesh, splitting his own bones. Once secured to the cross bar, the first prisoner was hoisted onto a pole, to which his feet were then nailed in like fashion. A sign above his head proclaimed him a robber, as the thief's own sign would.

Trying to block this gruesome image from his mind, the waiting prisoner turned to the crowd, searching for a friendly face to ease his fear. He began to cry for the family he had so disappointed, who would be shamed by his crucifixion. He cried for the pain to come, and he cried for what might happen to him after the pain stopped. Would this death be enough to pay for the life he had led?

An abrupt shout from those nearest the hilltop signalled that the next prisoner was about to be crucified. This was the Jew who had committed no crime. The prisoners knew it, and the passionate reaction of the crowd hinted that the people did too.

First the soldiers stripped him, then nailed him, silent, to the wood as they had the first prisoner. They hoisted him up and fastened a sign above him that read, "*THIS IS THE KING OF THE JEWS*," which brought a great cry of approval from some, and wailing from others. Many simply stood a distance away—waiting, grieving. Jesus himself made no sound except to pray, "*Father, forgive them, for they do not know what they are doing.*"

Now came the last prisoner, the thief, who watched Jesus very closely as the nails drove into his own hands and held him to the cross next to Jesus. It had not hurt quite as much as he had feared.

The thief had heard that the Jews hated Jesus because he claimed to be the Son of God, the Saviour, the promised Messiah. According to the prison gossip, the Jewish leaders considered this claim to be some kind of a scam, but the other prisoners could not see that it was anything deserving death. Yet here was this Jesus, while being tortured, praying for God to forgive the very people who were killing him without cause! Wanting to understand, the thief rallied his failing wits about him.

He saw that the more prominent in the crowd—the rulers—sneered at Jesus with the most venom. "You saved others; save yourself if you are the Christ, God's chosen one," they laughed up at him. Jesus said nothing. And with a clear view of the face of Jesus, the thief saw that he did not even react with unspoken anger or fear. Instead, his eyes brimmed with forgiveness.

Then the other criminal joined in with the crowd. From his cross on the right, he taunted Jesus sarcastically, *"Aren't you the Christ? Save yourself and us!"*

At these words, the thief felt an anger like he had never felt before. It was born of reverence for the man who hung next to him, and of a fleeting hope that this Jesus could somehow save him. Perhaps Jesus would ask God to forgive him too.

"Don't you fear God," he groaned to the other criminal, "since you have been given the very same sentence that Jesus has? Yet you and I are getting what our deeds deserve, while *this man has done nothing wrong."*

Then the thief looked at the "KING OF THE JEWS" and dared to say, *"Jesus, remember me when you come into your kingdom."*

Jesus answered him, *"I tell you the truth, today you will be with me in paradise."*

The thief gasped with surprise and relief. He had never experienced such joy in his whole self-serving life. This was the last thing he had expected to hear on the day he was crucified.

Three painful hours later, Jesus lifted his head and called out in a loud voice, *"Father, into your hands I commit my spirit."* And then he breathed his last.

The thief lingered in this life for some time after Jesus died, his anticipation easing the physical pain. "Imagine," he marvelled, "that the Son of

God would die for the likes of me!" Then he too breathed his last, and met the Lord again in paradise.

Taken from: Luke 23:32–46.

From the Bible:

"Whoever believes in the Son has eternal life, but whoever rejects the Son will not see life, for God's wrath remains on him" (John 3:36).

The length of our days is seventy years—or eighty, if we have the strength; yet their span is but trouble and sorrow, for they quickly pass, and we fly away (Psalm 90:10).

He has also set eternity in the hearts of men (Ecclesiastes 3:11b).

Talking it over:

1. *What three things did the thief fear at this point in his life? Which of these fears lessened as the story progressed, and why?*

2. *What did the thief discover about Jesus in the course of this story? What difference did this discovery make in the way the thief thought about himself and about his life?*

3. *You have a soul that will live forever. Does that make you want to change anything about your life?*

Merely the flames of men

Long before sunrise, Polycarp's eyes flew open and he felt cold drops of sweat slide across his back into his bedclothes. He jerked his head up and stared at the pillow that moments ago in his dream had been consumed by a raging fire. Shivering and unable to shake the image of the flaming pillow, Polycarp stoked the real fire in the main room of the little farm house where he was staying, and then settled himself down before its heat, quietly pondering his dream.

There had certainly been a great deal of fire in Smyrna lately. Over the past few weeks many of the most devoted believers from the old pastor's flock had been killed by the authorities because they had refused to declare the Roman emperor to be Lord and God. These Christians had only one God—the Lord Jesus Christ—and they could worship no other even in pretense to save their own lives! So the angry crowds had killed them and had cheered as they died.

Polycarp's brethren awoke that morning to find their aged pastor still before the fire, deep in prayer. After he finished, he looked up at them calmly and said, "I am to be burned for Christ's sake." Then he told them about his dream.

Three days later the Roman soldiers came for him. When Polycarp heard of their arrival, he refused to flee, saying to his friends, "I submit to God's will." He cheerfully ordered the Roman soldiers to be fed, and they agreed to let him pray for a time unharmed. For two hours he asked God's blessing for all those he had known and for the strength of Christ's Church. Side by side, the waiting soldiers and the grieving brethren paid silent reverence to this man's great faith.

Then the soldiers took Polycarp to the stadium in Smyrna and delivered him to the justice of the peace. Inside the arena, hundreds of excited citizens clamoured, "Bring in Polycarp, the father of the blasphemers, who keeps many from worshipping our gods or making sacrifices even to Caesar!"

The justice of the peace pleaded with Polycarp to worship Caesar so that the crowd would not demand his death. "Just say, 'Lord Caesar!' and offer a little sacrifice to him," he suggested. "You don't have to mean it. Then you can go on your way a free man, doing what you always do."

After many such pleas from the Roman official, Polycarp said only, "No, I will not even pretend to worship Caesar." So the guards led him into the arena.

The crowd screamed approval when they saw Polycarp enter, but over the tumult Polycarp and those near him heard a firm voice from above, saying, "Be strong, Polycarp, and play the man." Then he walked to where the proconsul stood waiting for him.

"Are you the great Bishop Polycarp?" the proconsul asked him, mocking.

"I am Polycarp."

"Swear your allegiance to Caesar," the proconsul demanded, "and you will go free. Renounce Christ."

"Eighty-six years I have served Christ, and he has done me no wrong; now I can do him no wrong. How can I renounce my Saviour and King?" cried Polycarp.

"I will feed you to my wild beasts if you don't swear to Caesar!"

"Bring them," said Polycarp.

"If you are not afraid of the wild beasts, I will have you consumed with fire unless you deny Christ."

Polycarp responded quickly and compassionately. "Oh, if only you could see that this fire you threaten me with is but a cold flicker in comparison to the everlasting fire with which God will punish for eternity those who do not follow Jesus Christ. I cannot deny him!"

And so Polycarp confessed himself to belong to Christ, and was burned alive by the pagans and the Jews in the Smyrna arena on what historians believe was February 23 in the year A.D. 155. As the flames crept near him, Polycarp was heard thanking God that he was deemed worthy to be martyred for the cause of Christ, and asking the Lord to receive his soul into his eternal presence.

From the Bible:

"Do not be afraid of those who kill the body but cannot kill the soul. Rather, be afraid of the One who can destroy both soul and body in hell" (Matthew 10:28).

"What good will it be for a man if he gains the whole world, yet forfeits his soul?" (Matthew 16:26a)

Talking it over:

1. *Give one reason Polycarp could not deny Christ to save his own life. (Hint: Polycarp revealed it when he said, "Eighty-six years I have served Christ, and he has done me no wrong....How can I renounce my Saviour and King?")*

2. *Polycarp understood that the life he was living in his earthly body was but a moment of his total life. As with all men, he had a soul that would live on for eternity. How do you think knowing this truth helped Polycarp during this test?*

3. *What do you think Polycarp would have done differently if he had not been thinking about his soul?*

The Fall of man

Questions to learn:

21. In what condition did God make Adam and Eve?
He made them holy and happy.

22. Did Adam and Eve stay holy and happy?
No. They sinned against God.

23. What is sin?
Sin is either transgressing the Law of God, or falling short of it.*

24. What is meant by transgression?
Doing what God forbids.

■　　■　　■

The day Adam and Eve fell from holiness and happiness was a tragic one. Their transgression of God's command would have such far-reaching consequences, both for their own lives and for the lives of billions of people to come. David Brainerd used the catechism questions about Adam and Eve's fall to teach American Indians about original and inherited sin. By this teaching, God brought many Indians to Christ.

* This answer originally read: "Sin is any transgression of the law of God."

"Where are you, Adam?"

Eve walked along the huge exposed root of a tree until she could touch the velvety wing of a large butterfly, flexing and folding on the tree's rugged bark.

"What did you call this one, Adam?" she asked the tall man beside her.

"I called that a tigerfly because of the stripes it has," he said, bending down and urging the little creature to light on his finger.

"The name fits," Eve said, delighted.

Adam then released the fluttering butterfly and beckoned Eve on through the plush grass.

Laughing, she followed. But when they came to the centre of the garden, Eve stopped short, her mouth open and her eyes wide. Adam took her hand.

Before them were the two most unusual trees in the garden. One, larger than any of the other trees, had a tremendous canopy. Eve thought they could live under it, so massive was its reach. Hanging on the many branches of this tree sparkled large round fruit that were plump and inviting.

The other tree was smaller but no less appealing. Its leaves were of many colours, the deepest hues of green, yellow and orange that Eve had seen. Its vivid fruit were much smaller than those of the other tree, but somehow promised a flavour at least as sweet and juicy.

"What are *these* Adam?" Eve asked in wonder.

"These are the two trees that God named specially. The larger one he calls the tree of life, and the smaller one is named the tree of the knowledge of good and evil." As he spoke, Eve rushed forward, wondering whether she should first reach for the fruit of the tree of life, or the smaller fruit of the second tree.

"Stop!" Adam demanded, which he had never done before. Eve was so stunned that she almost fell. She turned obediently and looked at him, surprised.

"We may not eat from the smaller tree," Adam instructed her. "God said to me, '*You are free to eat from any tree in the garden; but you must not eat from the tree of the knowledge of good and evil, for when you eat of it you will surely die.*'"

Eve considered his words, and was content with this single limitation of their freedom.

Then one day she came upon the trees while walking alone. She gazed on their beauty and began to reach for a fruit on the tree of life—the one she was allowed to eat from—when a rustling of leaves on the second tree caught her attention. There, on the length of a very long branch, was a bright, beautiful snake. At the end of the branch that the snake rested upon hung the largest and sweetest smelling fruit on the tree of knowledge.

The snake spoke softly to Eve.

"Did God really say, 'You must not eat from any tree in the garden'?"

Eve thought for a moment. Is that what Adam had told her? Would God have put such a restriction on them? No, God had only forbidden their eating from the one tree. Or had he? Yes, that was it.

"We may eat from any of the trees except the one you rest on," she said. But now feeling the slightest bit deprived by this, she added, "In fact, I believe he said that we may not even touch that one, or else we will die."

For a few moments, the snake said nothing. Eve saw, however, that it was quite indignant on her behalf. "Hmmm," she thought, "the snake is sorry for us. It might be very hard never even to touch the tree. Why, I could slip and fall against it as I pass, and then I would die."

Finally, the snake whispered to Eve so that she had to come very close to the branch to hear him. The sweetness of the fruit filled her nostrils.

"You will not die if you eat," it said.

That would be very nice, for Eve now wanted both to eat the fruit and to live.

"Rather," whispered the snake, *"when you eat of it your eyes will be opened, and you will be like God, knowing good and evil.* He told you not to eat—that you would die if you did—because he doesn't want you to know."

"Yes," Eve thought, "I would like to know all that God knows and isn't telling us, especially if I can find out *and* live." Everything that the snake had said made sense to her. Eve took the fruit from the limb around which the snake was wound. She did not die when she touched it, so she took a bite.

The flavour did not disappoint her; Adam must have some too. She ran to find him and explained everything the snake had said in the most convincing way she knew. It had sounded so right to her; surely it would to Adam as well.

But it did not sound right to Adam, who could not forget the unmistakable command of the Lord. Still, here was his wife so plaintive, and somehow newly distant from him. With slow deliberation, Adam hushed the qualms in his mind, then grasped and bit into the fruit.

84

As he swallowed, Adam glanced around the garden to see if God had seen them eat the fruit. Perhaps God wouldn't know what they had done if they didn't tell him. They would hide for a while, and when they met with God next they would be nowhere near the two trees. As he and Eve headed into the thicket, Adam realized that he was naked and he was ashamed of his nakedness. Fear, sadness, and misery quietly overtook his heart.

"Adam, *where are you*?" called the Lord.

Taken from: Genesis 2:8–3:9.

From the Bible:

When tempted, no one should say, "God is tempting me." For God cannot be tempted by evil, nor does he tempt anyone; but each one is tempted when, by his own evil desire, he is dragged away and enticed. Then, after desire has conceived, it gives birth to sin; and sin, when it is full-grown, gives birth to death (James 1:13–15).

To Adam he said, "Because you listened to your wife and ate from the tree about which I commanded you, 'You must not eat of it,' cursed is the ground because of you;…By the sweat of your brow you will eat your food until you return to the ground, since from it you were taken; for dust you are and to dust you will return" (Genesis 3:17a,19).

Talking it over:

1. *How did Adam and Eve feel about God, themselves and each other before Eve began to talk to the snake?*

2. *After he had sinned, how did Adam feel about God and himself?*

3. *Was Adam tricked into sinning as Eve was? Then why did he sin? (He willfully disregarded God's command.)*

David Brainerd and his catechized Indians

The young preacher rested his catechism primer on his upraised knee, supported by the breadth of an old maple log. In the flickering firelight, 24 buck-skinned figures were gathered round the clearing.

"And so even though Adam and Eve had a holy and peaceful life in the Garden of Eden, they disobeyed the command God had given them. Do you remember what happened to our first parents once they had sinned?" David Brainerd asked through his translator. He stared into the glistening faces before him, hoping that one or two were beginning to understand.

A weathered wisp of an Indian man stood up, his voice crackling with age. "They could no longer be holy and cheerful. They became sinful and miserable," were the words David heard as the Indian's answer was translated into English.

"Yes," David soberly answered. "Then all of us—red and white—who are Adam's children and grandchildren were born sinful and in a miserable state. Our nature is to sin from birth, and we cannot stop it or help it. But on each of us for every sin, God Almighty's anger rests. 'He is angry with the wicked every day,' as the Psalmist says."

David watched the effect of his words ripple over the faces of both young and old. Many nodded in agreement. Others scowled miserably at the truth. Then from the shadows, a tall, muscular Indian stepped forward.

"Pastor David, may I speak?" David nodded as the man moved lithely through his fellows. They looked somewhat blankly at him, wondering what he could be about. The man, a tribal leader of about 40, had long been one of the more free-spirited in the small village, giving little heed to his course. Yet lately he had often come to David's services.

"Pastor," he began. "You have said many times that before we come to Christ for salvation, we must see ourselves as helpless and unable ever to save ourselves by our own deeds."

His voice intensified. "I tried and tried to walk myself into this frame of mind, so that God might see me and approve of what I'd done and save me. I thought he would be pleased that I had come to see my sin and misery, and would judge me worthy of life eternal." The man paused, tears welling up in his eyes. "But pastor, over many days, when my heart walked into this frame

of mind, I could not see God pleased with me for knowing my sinful state. No. When I saw that there was no goodness in me, I knew that he was right to send me to hell, that it would be forever impossible for me to deserve God's pity for my soul."

"Yes," David agreed. "We can never save ourselves by any work of our own—even by the act of confessing ourselves unworthy. Since Adam and Eve's fall, our best thoughts are sinful and miserable indeed. And we are never worthy of any help from God." Here he paused and held out his arms toward the sad and weary man. His voice softened. "But, I invite you, and all sinners here, to come to Christ empty and alone, having nothing in you to deserve his acceptance. We must seek him and plead for mercy."

The man and his companions seemed to hang on David's words. He was encouraged because they had listened more and more attentively each day that he had, by turns, afflicted and comforted their souls with the Scriptures. A few moments later, the man interrupted again.

"Pastor," he said eagerly, "just now, with my heart, I saw something so good and bright that the words will not come." His voice quickened. "It steals away my heart whether I will it or no! My heart goes away of itself to this glory!"

Later David would write in his journal of this Indian man who had continued in his faith in Christ, left off bad habits, and become a growing Christian. And not only he, but many Indians of that tribe, came to know Christ through the preaching and catechizing of doctrine by David Brainerd. As David wrote in his journal on January 18, 1746:

> This method of instruction [teaching doctrine by the questions and answers of the catechism] I find very profitable. When I first entered upon it, I was exercised with fears lest my discourses would unavoidably be so doctrinal, that they would tend only to enlighten the head, but not to affect the heart. But the event proved quite otherwise; for these exercises have hitherto been remarkably blessed. [5]

From the Bible:

As it is written: "There is no-one righteous, not even one; there is no-one who understands, no-one who seeks God. All have turned away, they have together become worthless; there is no-one who does good, not even one" (Romans 3:10–12).

At one time we too were foolish, disobedient, deceived and enslaved by all kinds of passions and pleasures....But when the kindness and love of God our Saviour appeared, he saved us, not because of righteous things we had done, but because of his mercy (Titus 3:3a,4–5a).

[F]or all have sinned and fall short of the glory of God (Romans 3:23).

Talking it over:

1. *What is sin?*

2. *How did David Brainerd teach the Indians what sin was? How did knowing about Adam and Eve help the Indians understand their own sin?*

3. *What good did God eventually bring from the Indians' understanding of original sin (Adam and Eve's) and their own sin? How did God do this?*

Disbelieving God

Questions to learn:

25. What was the sin of our first parents?

Eating the forbidden fruit.

26. Why did they eat the forbidden fruit?

Because they did not believe what God had said.

27. Who tempted them to this sin?

The devil tempted Eve, and she gave the fruit to Adam.

■　■　■

Just as Adam and Eve demonstrated in the garden, sin always follows when we fail to believe God. The Israelites did not believe that God could truly give them the land of plenty he had first promised to Abraham centuries before. Their resulting refusal to enter Canaan had disastrous consequences for an entire generation of God's people. The fourteenth-century pre-Reformation teacher and writer, John Wycliffe, lived at a time in history when many people who professed to be Christians had slipped into sinful, unbelieving ways.

The seed of rebellion

Through a crevice between two boulders, Joshua and Caleb peered across the plush, green valley. On the hill opposite sat Hebron, a large city fortified by a tall, thick exterior wall and guarded by many sentries. The road leading up to the main gate was crowded with day labourers and families on their way to market. Caleb could see three or four shrines built on the high places within the city walls. This was where they displayed the idols they worshipped.

"Joshua, I just can't wait until our Lord topples those heathen shrines and delivers Hebron and all of Canaan into our hands!"

"It will surely be a glorious day, Caleb. Did you see the size of the grapes and pomegranates in the Valley of Eshcol? Why, there was enough juice in one fruit to quench my thirst for a whole day! We must take some back with us."

"Yes, we've seen enough. This land that the Lord has promised to us truly flows with milk and honey. Let's return and tell the others."

So Joshua rounded up the exploration party and they took some of the mammoth fruit from the Valley of Eshcol back to the many thousands of Israelites waiting for them at Kadesh in the Desert of Paran.

As soon as Moses got word of their coming, he called the people together to receive the spies' report about the land God had promised to their ancestor Abraham hundreds of years before. After waiting 40 days for them to return, a few hours did not seem too long for him to spend gathering the people into tribes around some large rocks from which the twelve could be heard.

Shaphat spoke first. "The land is truly bountiful. Here is the fruit to prove it," he said, holding up a huge branch full of figs.

"But," said Gaddiel in a shaky voice, "the people of Canaan are just as strong and large as what grows there. Why, in comparison to them we seemed like mere grasshoppers."

Caleb shot a look of alarm at Joshua as the people began to murmur. This was not at all how they had perceived things. Sure the Canaanites were healthy and numerous, but they were no obstacle for the living God.

Caleb waved down the many voices rising in indignation and fear. He turned to Moses and said firmly so that all could hear, "We should go in and take possession of the land, for we can surely do it if the Lord leads us."

But Ammiel, standing behind Caleb on the rocks, shouted to the people: "We can't attack those people because they are much too strong. All those we saw were like giants. They would devour us!"

Someone in the crowd—one of the elders—spoke aloud what many were grumbling under their breaths. "Why did God bring us here only to let us be slaughtered by the Canaanites? We would be better off as slaves back in Egypt. Let's choose a leader to take us back there."

"No!" thundered Joshua. "The land we explored is exceedingly good. If the Lord is pleased with us, he will lead us into Canaan and will give it to us. Don't be afraid of the Canaanites, because the Lord will swallow them up. We must not rebel in unbelief. Trust his promises."

"Stone him!" screamed the elder, and several men started to scramble up the rocks to seize Joshua and kill him for saying what they did not want to hear.

Suddenly a cloud appeared to all the Israelites, and the Lord was within it.

"Moses! How long will these stiff-necked people refuse to believe me, in spite of all the miracles I have performed on their behalf? They have tested me ten times since I delivered them out of slavery, and still they grumble and disbelieve my promises. I have provided them water out of rocks, food has dropped to them out of the sky and appeared as dew each morning for their taking, and their enemies have been swallowed up in a raging sea. Now their unbelief has thwarted their obedience to the very purpose for which I brought them here," came the mighty voice of God. "No more!"

As the people wept and cowered beneath the cloud, Moses fell on his face and pleaded with the Lord to pardon the Israelites yet again.

"Very well, Moses. I have forgiven them once again as you have asked. But as surely as my glory fills the Earth, not one of these disbelieving people for whom I have miraculously provided will enter the plentiful land that I promised to their forefathers. Rather, they will wander in this desert for 40 years, and all who are age 20 and over will die in the desert except for my faithful servants Caleb and Joshua. When all the others are gone, these two will lead the next generation into my Promised Land."

Taken from: Numbers 13:1–14:35.

From the Bible:

Who were they who heard and rebelled? Were they not all those Moses led out of Egypt? And with whom was [God] angry for forty years? Was it not with those who sinned, whose bodies fell in the desert? And to whom did God swear that they would never enter his rest if not to those who disobeyed? So we see that they were not able to enter, because of their unbelief (Hebrews 3:16–19).

Talking it over:

1. *What was the sin of the Israelites in the above story? Why did they commit this sin?*

2. *How was their sin the same as that of Adam and Eve in the garden?*

3. *Does failing to trust God result in disobedience? Why?*

4. *When we know and believe God's promises, what will we do? (Consider Caleb's actions.)*

One man's crusade against disbelief

Into the towns and shires of England, the Roman Catholic Church sent an army of friars calling the people to a crusade against the French. It seemed that by some ballot-casting tomfoolery of the higher-ups, there were suddenly *two* heads of the Church instead of *one*. Now Pope Urban VI—the one favoured by most of the English—was calling for a crusade against the other pope, Clement VII, who was favoured by the French. Wherever the messengers went, the scene in the English villages was always much the same.

A friar from the nearest monastery would arrive wearing a robe of the finest cloth draped over a great, satisfied belly. His personal secretary would follow close behind, waving the papers from Rome that gave the friar full authority to raise money and arms for what was referred to as the pope's "holy cause." With a flash of these papers, they would silence any objections of the parish priest, and then they would march through the town calling the people to hear the decree of the *good* pope—Urban.

"Hear ye, hear ye," the secretary would shout as the people flocked into the square from their shops and fields, homes and taverns. The assembled crowd was always a tattered lot, hungry and ill-tempered, but ever malleable to the demands of a powerful Church. The secretary would continue in his best stage voice:

> His Holiness, Urban VI—the true pope, Bishop of Rome in the direct lineage of Saint Peter—calls all God-fearing persons within the realm of England to take up arms against the French usurper who masquerades as Clement VII and falsely claims the highest office on earth. This is a crusade! Go forth as soldiers of God and defend the Holy Roman See. Women, send your husbands, fathers, and sons, and attain for them the Church's assurance of God's forgiveness of their sins. Men, rally your brothers and march off to this holy war just as your noble ancestors 200 years ago marched to Palestine in defense of God's kingdom on earth. Be assured that you will see heaven instantly if you die in valour on God's battlefield.

Each of you must also give of your possessions according to your ability. The sincerity of your penance is surely evident in the amount of your gift. Remember that God sees, and so does the Church that administers his grace. We would hate to have to deny God's forgiveness to a courageous soldier because of the unbelief of a greedy wife. And so, we warn you, dig deep.

These promises of violent glory and threats of hell did much to motivate the illiterate people of this day. Men went off to the crusade simply because a pope said it was a holy, noble thing to do. They had been taught that the Roman Church alone knew the mind of God. They did not and could not read the Bible to find out what it said of these things, nor did the Roman Church want the Bible preached in a language the masses could understand. And so, the people were blind to the fact that the Church often manipulated them like animals, holding hell over their heads to gain their lands and possessions. Indeed, the Roman Church was the richest entity in the land, while those it served grew increasingly poorer.

One Englishman, however, was not blind to the Roman Church's sins. His name was John Wycliffe. By the time the pope called for the English to crusade against the French in 1383, Wycliffe was a 54-year-old invalid who was forced to live out his days as the parish priest in a small hamlet called Lutterworth. From Lutterworth, he spoke out against the crusade as an outrageous example of the Church's unbelief.

Wycliffe had first discovered the errors of the Roman Church while studying theology at Oxford University. There he saw that the Church lacked esteem for God's Word, and that this failure had led it into all sorts of sin. When he had become a professor of theology, Wycliffe had spoken out condemning many of these sins, chief among them the Roman Church leaders' lust for power and wealth. He was especially critical of the monks, who had long ago given up their simple, cloistered lifestyles and now spent their energies overseeing rich estates. Wycliffe also had preached against the papacy, whose main concern was to control kings rather than to point people to Christ. And he had even challenged the Church's teachings, many of which were simply superstitions used to control the people like puppets.

In short, Wycliffe had seen that the so-called Church of his day did not believe or obey what Christ had said. "Feed my sheep," Jesus had instructed the disciples. Instead, the medieval Roman Church did all it could to deprive them of nourishment, both spiritual and physical. And sin abounded.

In response to Wycliffe's charges, Church authorities had labelled him a heretic. He was excommunicated and driven from Oxford. His books were burned. And those who preached his views were threatened with imprisonment and torture.

Not long after the crusaders returned home, beaten and dejected, John Wycliffe died in Lutterworth. But he left his English brethren a Bible crudely translated into the tongue of the people. He also left behind a good number of Englishmen who shared his vision to preach God's Word, exposing sin and unbelief. Several generations of these preachers—referred to as "Lollards"—travelled throughout the English countryside, evading the spies of both pope and king, preaching from John Wycliffe's sermons and English Bible, and feeding Christ's sheep. They were still preaching 140 years later when God sent a whole army of reformers to convict the faithless medieval Church of its unbelief. As an early prophet of this movement, John Wycliffe is known as the "Morning Star" of the Reformation.

From the Bible:

See to it, brothers, that none of you has a sinful, unbelieving heart that turns away from the living God (Hebrews 3:12).

Rather, we have renounced secret and shameful ways; we do not use deception, nor do we distort the word of God. On the contrary, by setting forth the truth plainly we commend ourselves to every man's conscience in the sight of God (2 Corinthians 4:2).

Talking it over:

1. *Did the medieval Church in John Wycliffe's day believe God? What actions show its unbelief?*

2. *According to the Hebrews passage above, is it sin to disbelieve God? Why?*

3. *Can you think of a time when you didn't believe God and were led into sin?*

4. *Why should we believe God? (Because he's true and he is sovereign over history and creation. His Word is trustworthy and is always right.)*

Inherited sinful nature

Questions to learn:

28. What happened to our first parents when they had sinned?

Instead of being holy and happy, they became sinful and miserable.

29. What effect had the sin of Adam on all mankind?

All mankind is born in a state of sin and misery.

30. What do we inherit from Adam as a result of this original sin?

A sinful nature.

31. What does every sin deserve?

The anger and judgment of God.

■ ■ ■

Cain's murder of his brother Abel, mentioned in Genesis 4, shows how quickly and thoroughly Adam's sin in Genesis 3 afflicted the next generations. Augustine was a leader from early church history who had deep insight into Adam's sin and its effect on the whole human race.

Like father, like son

"It's not fair," Cain muttered, as he swung his gunnysack over one shoulder and set out down the familiar path. Ever since he had learned to farm, he'd been fighting thorns and thistles just to get a few spindly plants to grow. It was only by sweat and strain that he had harvested these few extra vegetables for the altar.

Cain recalled the stories his father Adam had told about the lush foliage that grew so abundantly in the garden he had first tended. Life must have been so simple then!

But, Cain thought resentfully, after a time God had cursed the ground and had thrown his parents out of the beautiful garden. These days, it seemed to him, life was nothing but work, work, work.

"Now this God wants me to sacrifice to him part of my own hard-earned produce, even though he is the one who makes it so difficult for us," Cain grumbled, as he spotted his brother Abel just ahead of him on the path leading to the family altar. Grudgingly, Cain followed, and then stood silent and frowning as Abel laid his firstborn lamb of the season on the hot coals and watched the flames consume it.

When it was his turn, Cain propped his vegetables carelessly over the coals, wondering how long he would keep going through the motions of this ritual. His father had dared to disobey God; he wondered if he would ever have the courage to do the same. He waited by the altar for several minutes, increasingly anxious to get back to his fields before the day grew too old, but his vegetables remained cold and limp on the glowing coals. He stoked and stoked, but could not get the fire to kindle them. His offering was being refused.

"This is just too much," Cain said angrily. "He won't even accept my gift."

Just then a voice rumbled over the smoking altar. *"Why are you angry? Why is your face downcast? If you do what is right, will you not be accepted? But if you do not do what is right, sin is crouching at your door; it desires to have you, but you must master it."*

At this rebuke, Cain simply turned on his heels and stalked away. "Fine," he thought, "Abel's offering is okay, but mine is not. It's just not fair."

Later, however, as Abel started back toward the hills to tend his flocks, Cain followed him.

"Come out into the country with me, brother," he urged, a plan taking shape in his mind. After all, his father had dared, now why not him?

"All right," said Abel. "I have a little time to spare."

As Abel innocently followed his brother into the field, Cain attacked and killed him. "There," Cain fumed, watching Abel's life ebb away, "you won't be making me look bad at the altar any more." And the world's first murder was complete.

But again the voice of the Lord sought and found Cain, this time to curse rather than to warn him: *"What have you done? Listen! Your brother's blood cries out to me from the ground. Now you are under a curse and driven from the ground, which opened its mouth to receive your brother's blood from your hand....You will be a restless wanderer on the earth."*

So God took away even the livelihood that Cain had once had tilling the soil. And thereafter, day by day, person by person, the world that had once known beauty and innocence grew more violent and futile and fallen.

Taken from: Genesis 4:1–16.

From the Bible:

"For I desire mercy, not sacrifice, and acknowledgment of God rather than burnt offerings. Like Adam, they have broken the covenant—they were unfaithful to me there" (Hosea 6:6–7).

All of us also lived among [the disobedient] at one time, gratifying the cravings of our sinful nature and following its desires and thoughts. Like the rest, we were by nature objects of wrath (Ephesians 2:3).

Talking it over:

1. *Why did Cain kill Abel? What attitudes did he have that led him to murder his brother?*

2. *Where did Cain get his tendency toward sinful thoughts and actions?*

3. *Does Adam give anything to us today? How do you know?*

The pear tree incident

"Everyone, come on! Over here, across the road!"

"Look at those!"

Into the quiet North African night broke the shouts of a gang of youths swaggering along the outside wall of a pear orchard. Their laughter echoed starkly against the town's dark, empty streets.

"We're almost to your house, Augustine. Are your pears as big as this?" joked one boy, pointing to the shadow cast in their path by a clump of the huge fruit shimmering in the moonlight.

"Bigger," answered the dark youth carelessly. "And twice as tasty."

"Have you tried them to see?" taunted the first boy.

"No, but I could if I would," said Augustine. "Dare me if you will."

"Wait, I've a better idea," a third boy urged. "Let's climb this wall and drag down these pears. We've no other plan for the evening."

"Done!" cried all the others, as they lunged for the nearest branches. The furious sound of scuffling soon gave way to snapping twigs and thudding pears. Unconcerned with hiding their deeds, the boys worked on amidst their own laughter. Pear after pear jerked and fell. Any neighbor who overheard the gang's clatter feared the size of the group too much to challenge their rowdy behaviour. And so, in a short time, the boys succeeded in amassing large piles of clumsily harvested pears.

"Now, what will we do?" asked the boy who had first suggested the scheme. "I'm not hungry for these bruised things." They all gazed at the dark clumps in the dirt.

"I know, let's take them to the hogs," Augustine answered. "That will get rid of them." And so they did.

Years later, as a grown man, this same Augustine repented of his past sins and was miraculously converted to Christianity under the influence of the early church leaders like Ambrose of Milan. In the year A.D. 397, he became the bishop of the church in an Egyptian town called Hippo, and through his writings God used him to help bring the Christian faith to many in Europe.

After he had been bishop for a number of years, Augustine heard about a British church official named Pelagius who was enticing hopeful converts with a false teaching about human nature. People found the new teaching

much easier to accept than the gospel truth that God had given the apostles. Augustine and Pelagius became fierce opponents.

"We are not sinners at birth," taught Pelagius. "Adam's sin does not affect us. Adam was a bad example for us, but there is no link between his sin and us. It's possible for anyone to keep from sinning for his whole life, as in fact some besides Jesus have. The ability to be saved through personal righteousness is within every man. We have only to choose."

"No!" Augustine recoiled when he heard this. "Our souls were profoundly ruined from the time of Adam's fall. He represented the human race and the whole race fell with him." Augustine recalled from his boyhood the incident of the pear trees, when he had stolen, not because he was hungry or because he had no pears of his own. He had stolen simply for his enjoyment of the crime itself. He did it for sheer wickedness' sake. Evil was in him. So Augustine challenged Pelagius with the truth that we cannot do anything on our own that is righteous in God's sight. Nothing less than a saving act of God's grace and mercy through Christ's sacrifice can change our wicked hearts—a wickedness that has been passed down to us from the time of Adam.

"Even though the pear tree sin was ugly, I relished committing it," Augustine later confessed. He said that he had loved stripping the trees of their fruit, not because he loved the pears, but because he loved the destruction itself. When he thought about his own heart, Augustine knew that it was not innocent. And he also knew that if he believed the lie that Pelagius taught—that he was innocent in his own heart—he would love God less because he would not see his need for God's mercy through Christ. "Who can help me, other than he who penetrates the dark places of my heart with his brilliant light?" Augustine asked. [6]

He knew that sin resides in all men and women because of what Adam did. Each person sins for the sake of sinning and cannot please God unless Christ changes his or her heart. So God used the pear tree in Augustine's life to teach him about what Adam's sin meant to him and to all people. Augustine's writings on these subjects discredited Pelagian teaching and have been studied by Christians throughout the centuries to help them understand the meaning of original sin.

From the Bible:

Therefore, just as sin entered the world through one man, and death through sin, and in this way death came to all men, because all sinned…But the gift is not like the trespass. For if the many died by the trespass of the one man, how much more did God's grace and the gift that came by the grace of the one man, Jesus Christ, overflow to the many! …For just as through the disobedience of the one man the many were made sinners, so also through the obedience of the one man the many will be made righteous (Romans 5:12,15,19).

If we claim to be without sin, we deceive ourselves and the truth is not in us (1 John 1:8).

Talking it over:

1. *What happened to every future person when Adam sinned?*

2. *What shows that we each have a sinful nature? In our own power can we decide and choose never to sin? Why?*

3. *What tempts us to sin? (Thoughts of pleasure, but also an inherent wayward bent to want to sin.) After the initial pleasure that we feel our sin brings, what happens?*

UNIT 3

ATONEMENT

Regeneration

Questions to learn:

32. Can anyone go to heaven with this sinful nature?

No. Our hearts must be changed before we can be fit for heaven.

33. What is a change of heart called?

Regeneration.

34. Who can change a sinner's heart?

The Holy Spirit alone.

35. What is righteousness?

It is God's goodness.

36. Can anyone be saved by his own righteousness?

No. No one is good enough for God.

■　■　■

Only God can change our hearts so that we can love and obey him. Though Saul was convinced at first that men could only find favour with God by obeying every letter of God's Law, God regenerated Saul's heart and gave him a righteousness that came by faith. The eighteenth-century preacher John Wesley also tried to reach God through his own pious practices, but learned that only by sharing in Christ's righteousness can we please the Lord.

Former Christian "Enemy Number One"

Saul of Tarsus was an upstanding Jewish Pharisee. He devoutly observed every custom, feast and sacrifice that had been practiced by God's people in Old Testament times. And, like most good Pharisees, he was furious about the many Jews who had recently forsaken the Law of Moses to follow a man named Jesus, who they claimed was the Messiah that God had promised.

"What a scheme—trying to pass off an uneducated carpenter as the Messiah!" Saul said to himself. "Why, what they really are seeking after is nothing more than an excuse to discard righteousness. Under their scheme, every sort of vile sinner could find his way to God without even obeying God's Law. This is nothing but an insult to religion!"

Like the other Pharisees, Saul had fully expected the nonsense swirling around about Jesus to cease on the day they had crucified him. But when Jesus' followers soon came up with that story about his being resurrected, Saul knew that they were dealing with a very crafty lot. Clearly they would stop at nothing to trick their fellow Jews into ignoring God's Law. He simply could not allow this to happen.

So Saul became the self-proclaimed "Enemy Number One" of the Jesus followers.

The stoning of Stephen in Jerusalem had shown him what had to be done. Saul had been shocked that any of the blasphemers were willing to suffer for their charade, much less die for it. Recalling the scene almost made Saul sick. There Stephen was, broken and bleeding amidst a pile of rocks, gazing at the sky and crying out in self-righteous concern, "Lord, Jesus, don't hold their sin against them." Imagine him asserting that the Pharisees were sinning by protecting God's Law from the twisted notions of Stephen and his friends!

Looking down at the broken body of Stephen, Saul had pledged to himself and God that he would crush every single one of them. And he had set about doing just that, going from house to house arresting disciples, having them thrown into the prisons of Jerusalem and put to death.

During this time, many of those being persecuted left Jerusalem. But wherever they went, they preached that Jesus is the Son of God, and people believed.

One morning in the midst of his crusade against the disciples, Saul was headed to Damascus, where he was sure he would find more followers of Jesus. He had letters with him from the High Priest authorizing him to arrest any that he came across and bring them back to Jerusalem. With him were servants and certain other Pharisees of like mind.

As he neared Damascus that afternoon, the day suddenly flashed many times brighter than the sun. Saul shut his eyes but the dazzling light overpowered him, and he fell to the ground and covered his head.

"Saul, Saul, why do you persecute me?" said a voice out of the brightness.

"Could this be the God of my fathers?" Saul wondered. But why did God say that Saul—one of his most devoted servants—was persecuting him? Saul answered, *"Who are you, Lord?"*

"I am Jesus, whom you are persecuting. Now get up and go into the city, and you will be told what you must do."

Saul lay on the ground in crumpled dejection. His insides twisted. Jesus? "Could Jesus be what he had claimed to be, the Messiah? Could he be the Son of God?" Saul wondered. "If so, what have I done?" His baffled companions peered down at him with concern.

Those standing nearest picked the shattered man up out of the dust. He opened his eyes, but he could not see. So they took his hands and led him into Damascus, where he would most certainly not be imprisoning any disciples.

For three days Saul prayed. He ate nothing, drank nothing, and saw nothing, except a vision in which a man named Ananias came and placed his hands on Saul and restored his sight. Through it all, Saul prayed and waited.

On the third day Ananias came. He put his hands over Saul's eyes and said, "Brother, the Lord Jesus who spoke to you on the road has sent me to you. He gives you back your eyesight, and gives you spiritual sight for the first time. Be filled with his Holy Spirit."

As Ananias fell silent, something like scales dropped from Saul's eyes and he could see. Far better, from that moment Saul saw the truth about Jesus, who had filled him with the Holy Spirit. Saul was baptized and immediately began to preach the righteousness that comes only through the risen Christ.

Taken from: Acts 7:54–8:4; 9:1–19; 26:9–20.

From the Bible:

Even though I was once a blasphemer and a persecutor and a violent man, I was shown mercy because I acted in ignorance and unbelief. The grace of our Lord was poured out on me abundantly, along with the faith and love that are in Christ Jesus....Christ Jesus came into the world to save sinners—of whom I am the worst. But for that very reason I was shown mercy so that in me, the worst of sinners, Christ Jesus might display his unlimited patience as an example for those who would believe on him and receive eternal life (1 Timothy 1:13–16).

I want you to know, brothers, that the gospel I preached is not something that man made up. I did not receive it from any man, nor was I taught it; rather, I received it by revelation from Jesus Christ (Galatians 1:11–12).

Talking it over:

1. *At the beginning of the story, why did Saul think he did not need Christ in order to reach God? How did he think he would reach God?*

2. *What did Saul not understand about men's attempts to be righteous enough to reach God on their own?*

3. *What changed Saul's heart about his own righteousness? From the catechism questions, what is this change of heart called?*

No method will do

John Wesley brought the meeting of the Oxford Holy Club to order with a crack of his gavel on the heavy oak table in front of him. Though a small man, he was dignified and commanding, and his peers naturally looked to him as a leader. "I am pleased to announce that my brother Charles and I will set sail for America on October 14 to accompany General J.E. Oglethorpe to the new English colony of Georgia. We shall take the gospel of Christ to the Indian heathen nearby."

"What a splendid plan!" exclaimed George Whitefield, the newest and youngest member of the club.

"Yes," Charles agreed. "I was uneasy at first, but John has convinced me that we can please God greatly through missionary service, so we are going."

"But how will we get on without you?" asked James Hervey. "Why, John, you have been our very definition of holiness!"

"You will manage if you continue to carefully follow the methods of daily self-examination and holy living that I have prepared," John assured his friend. "And, James, I recall that you particularly are prone to cut short your Friday fast. We must be committed to our righteousness, gentlemen! Else, how will God recognize us as his own?"

On a Sunday evening four months later, John Wesley stood on the deck of the *Simmonds* in the midst of one of many storms that had blown them violently on their way toward Georgia. He clutched the doorframe of the cabin, and braced himself for an approaching wave that he saw would swallow the ship.

John had thought he could face death with assurance. Instead, panic seized him, while within the cabin, a small group of German missionaries —called Moravians—sang a Psalm to the Lord.

When the wave hit, the mighty wall of water split the mainsail into pieces, and poured through the ship. Unbelievably, however, when the water receded the *Simmonds* was still afloat. Over the splashing and creaking, John heard the terrified screams of his own countrymen alongside the calm, clear voices of the Moravians concluding their song.

The next day, John found one of the Germans and asked him, "Sir, weren't you afraid during the storm?"

"No, thanks be to God," he answered.

"But what about your women and children? Were they not afraid?"

"We are not afraid to die, my friend," the German answered. "We know that we will be with the Lord when we leave this world."

The Moravian's words plagued John throughout the months in Georgia as he preached not to Indians, but primarily to unruly settlers who had been relocated to the New World out of old, overcrowded English prisons. To his dismay, the flock that he was given in Savannah did not warm to the rigid rules for daily living and high standards of righteousness that John tried to impose. Soon he was the most unpopular man in town. Two years later he fled back to England to escape accusations against him by some of his church members.

On the voyage home, John thought about his own righteousness. Why had it not helped him to win souls to God? And why, despite his exemplary lifestyle, did he not know the peace described by the Moravian man he had questioned on the *Simmonds*? The only thing John knew for sure when he arrived in England early in 1738 was that his own brand of religion was lacking. All his good deeds and strict habits were but filthy rags hiding a tremendous sin of unbelief.

So God sent another Moravian to help John—the young preacher Peter Boehler. For three months, Peter ministered to and encouraged John Wesley with the truth of the gospel: that not by his own righteousness, but only by faith in the atoning work of Jesus Christ is someone saved from his sin, and that faith is itself a gift from God's Holy Spirit.

Early on May 24, John read in his Bible, "Thou art not far from the kingdom of God" (Mark 12:34, KJV). That afternoon he went to church and was touched by a hymn praising God for the mercy he shows to repentant sinners. Later that evening, he attended a meeting of some Christians in Aldersgate Street, and while one man described the change God works in a person's heart through belief in Christ, John felt his own heart "strangely warmed." He knew for the first time that Christ had indeed taken away *his* sins and given him a true righteousness not based on his own deeds. His whole heart had been changed.

Soon after that, John began the open-air preaching ministry that God would use to save many in England for his glory. For fifty years, John travelled throughout the British Isles on horseback and preached the salvation he now knew so well.

From the Bible:

[H]e saved us, not because of righteous things we had done, but because of his mercy. He saved us through the washing of rebirth and renewal by the Holy Spirit, whom he poured out on us generously through Jesus Christ our Saviour (Titus 3:5–6).

It does not, therefore, depend on man's desire or effort, but on God's mercy (Romans 9:16).

Talking it over:

1. *Why did John Wesley at first not have salvation even though he lived so righteously?*

2. *What did God have to convince John of before he could give him faith? Did John get this faith on his own?*

3. *How was John's heart changed?*

The covenant of grace

Questions to learn:

37. What is a covenant?

An agreement between two or more persons.

38. What is the covenant of grace?

The agreement God made with his elect people to save them from their sins.

39. What did Christ undertake in the covenant of grace?

To keep the whole Law for his people, and to suffer the punishment due to their sins.

■ ■ ■

Throughout history, men have attempted to add to the gospel of Christ, believing that they must contribute to their own salvation. The Bible tells us that even the apostle Peter became temporarily ensnared by such false beliefs. Imagine what it took to draw him away from the truth, and how he must have felt when Paul publicly exposed his error. By Martin Luther's day, in the sixteenth century, the Roman Catholic Church's distortions of the simple gospel had settled like a dark cloud over the covenant of grace, but the Holy Spirit led Luther to find the truth through his own prayerful study of God's Word.

One step back, three steps forward

A group of the faithful followers of Christ in Antioch reclined in the shade of a courtyard, sharing their morning meal. Peter, who had excused himself just before the meat was served, stood outside a window where he could not be seen. He longed to be in with them, but just couldn't risk being found actually eating with Gentiles—eating what Gentiles eat. If he got close enough, however, Peter could hear their voices.

"I understand that a group from the Jerusalem church is due here this evening," confided Barnabas to those gathered around the table nearest the window. Actually, Peter had been notified that the delegation from the Jerusalem church would arrive this morning, which was precisely why he was not inside breaking bread with his friends.

Peter alone knew why the delegation was coming—to address the threat that Gentile Christians posed to the Jewish laws. Some in the Jerusalem church wanted to make the Gentiles act like Jews, eating only acceptable foods, and following all the other rules and rituals that God had required of them before Christ had come. In part, these Jewish Christians hoped to maintain enough of their Jewish heritage to continue to be accepted into the synagogues and temple.

"Surely, preserving a few of the Jewish customs won't compromise the gospel," Peter tried to assure himself.

While pondering this matter, Peter's attention was drawn back to the courtyard by the mention of his own name. "Where's Peter?" asked a passionate, confident voice he recognized at once as Paul's.

No one said anything, but Peter detected the general rustling of shoulders shrugging in response. He strained to detect whether they were hurt by his absence or just confused by it. He could not tell.

At just that moment Peter felt a tap on his back, and swivelled abruptly to face the Jerusalem group. There stood their leader, smiling at Peter approvingly.

"Peter, we're so glad to hear that you are on our side. We cannot allow these Gentiles to run roughshod over God's Law," he said, as he looked in through the window and saw Paul eating forbidden meat next to Gentile believers.

"You betrayers of the Law!" he yelled into the courtyard. "Eating with uncircumcised Gentiles!"

The brothers in the courtyard froze, with their mouths full, as the delegation from Jerusalem entered, uninvited. "All you Gentiles must immediately obey our Jewish laws, including those about circumcision, what you eat, and how you prepare your food," their leader commanded. "How can you expect God to include you in the atonement of Jesus if you won't first follow his laws?"

The Antioch believers stared silently at their indignant visitors. Exasperated, the angry leader waved Peter into the courtyard. "Peter, tell them," he said.

Peter stuttered around for a moment or two, wondering what he should say. Why, just yesterday he had been here eating right alongside his Gentile friends, having discarded the ceremonial Jewish laws just as the rest of them had.

Finally Paul could bear it no longer. He jumped on top of the table he had been eating on and proclaimed, "No, my friends! Don't listen to them. We Jews know better than anyone that we cannot reach God through the Law, because none of us can obey it perfectly. God gave us the Law so that we would understand our sin and be convicted of our wrongdoing. But through the new covenant—the covenant of grace—we benefit by Christ's righteousness. He alone kept the whole Law perfectly. He is the fulfillment of God's covenant with us to save us from our sins. If these men are right, and we could be righteous by observing the Law, then Jesus would not have had to die for us. His sacrifice would have been in vain. But it is not so."

"If Peter truly believes what these men say, he has been hoodwinked," Paul told the Antioch brothers. "But in truth, I think he is simply being a hypocrite. He himself ate with us yesterday."

"How is it, Peter, that you now try to force these Gentiles to follow the Jewish customs that you do not?" Paul asked.

Paul's words stung Peter's tender conscience. Slowly his head began to clear. How could he have belittled the tremendous sacrifice of his Lord? Was not Jesus' death enough?

"Yes,…yes, Paul is right," he admitted humbly. "These men are trying to add onto the gospel of Christ. They would have you believe that we must deserve salvation by living a certain way, rather than rely on the simple, undeserved mercy of Christ alone. But we must face it, brothers," and here he turned to the men from Jerusalem, "we cannot get to God by our own effort. Our Lord's sacrifice was enough. Accept it, and rejoice!"

Taken from: Acts 15:1–11; Galatians 2:11–21.

From the Bible:

"Now then, why do you try to test God by putting on the necks of the disciples a yoke that neither we nor our fathers have been able to bear? No! We believe it is through the grace of our Lord Jesus that we are saved, just as they are" (Acts 15:10–11).

Those who want to make a good impression outwardly are trying to compel you to be circumcised. The only reason they do this is to avoid being persecuted for the cross of Christ (Galatians 6:12).

Talking it over:

1. *Some of the Jewish believers in Jerusalem were misleading the Gentiles by telling them that they couldn't have eternal life unless they followed certain Jewish rules. From the story and the Galatians passage, why might they have done this?*

2. *What is grace? (unmerited favour) What did Jesus do for us in the covenant of grace?*

3. *Are there any works that we must or can do to help us to gain God's forgiveness? (See also Ephesians 2:8–9.)*

The monk who couldn't measure up

Outside of Martin Luther's tiny tower room, crudely chiseled stone steps wound down to a large cavern where the other monks sat around several wooden tables eating their dinner of mutton, bread and water.

"Will Brother Luther join us tonight?" asked a young monk, as one of the others rang the dinner bell again for Luther. None of them really expected a reply, for Luther often studied while the others ate. As usual, tonight he ignored the summons and continued his reading. Many times he would go days without joining them for a single meal, locked in his barren room without sleeping or speaking to anyone. He often knelt or lay on his face for hours at a time praying for righteousness.

"He's a troubled young man," the monks whispered to one another. "Nothing satisfies him." And they were right.

As a monk, Luther had learned that he might hope to avoid God's wrath by devoting himself to fasting, praying, taking up collections for the Church, and participating in the Church's many rituals. Luther desperately wanted peace with God, and he pushed himself harder than any of the other monks to win God over with such behaviour. For he believed that if he did not try hard enough to be good, God would judge him unworthy of eternal life in heaven.

No matter how hard Luther had tried, however, he feared that his efforts fell far short of God's standard of righteousness. He found that he could not completely deny himself. He could not go long enough without eating or wanting to eat. He could not pray without stopping or letting his tired mind wander. Despite his enormous self-control, hateful thoughts about his fellow monks entered his mind and sometimes lingered there. Worst of all, when he had managed to be very good, he often felt himself superior to the others. At these times, Luther would torture his body and soul all the more, hoping his penance might soothe God's anger.

By now, however, Luther despaired of ever being able to gain God's favour. None of his good works was enough. He could never quite overcome all of his selfishness. He had done everything he knew to do, everything that the sixteenth-century Roman Church had taught him was necessary to attain salvation. According to the Church, he was okay. Yet where was the peace

that he so longed for? All he saw was God's mighty hand raised against him in judgment. And worse still, he knew that was what he deserved.

Day after day, Luther pored over the Bible hoping to find some comfort. There was something about salvation that he did not yet understand...something. Although his teachers had treated the Church's doctrines as more authoritative than the Bible itself, Luther was convinced that they had gotten something wrong. Had they added something that was not there or left out something important? So it was that in his searching he was led to the book of Romans.

In his tower room, the Holy Spirit gradually revealed to Luther the meaning of these words from Romans 1:17: "The just shall live by faith." The just shall live by faith.

Faith. Not rules. Not perfection. Not penance. Faith.

"That's it!" Luther realized. "I can never do enough good works to please God, or make myself suffer enough to appease him. What he commands instead is simply that I put my trust in the atoning work of the Lord Jesus Christ, who unlike me, was righteous by obeying the Father in all things, even unto death on the cross. He took my place. He took my sin. He gave me his righteousness. All the fasting, praying and rituals in the world cannot save my soul. It's a gift, by his grace! Why, he has even given me the faith to believe."

Finally Martin Luther had seen how contrary the teaching of the Roman Catholic Church of his day was to God's truth. Somehow, over the years, the medieval Church had slipped back into the old mindset that salvation depends in part on human effort. And the Church had set itself up as the judge of that effort—dictating what people had to do to win eternity, and claiming to have authority from God to grant salvation. Often, what the Church directed the people to do could not even be found in the Bible. In fact, many of these requirements were simply for the purpose of raising money, not saving souls.

God sent Luther with his newfound truth to knock on the Church's door and demand a return to the covenant of grace, based as it is solely on the worthiness of Christ's sacrifice on the cross. With Luther's careful teaching, many people of his day and since have understood that entry into this covenant with God does not depend on our own works, no matter how zealous.

From the Bible:

"This is the covenant I will make with the house of Israel after that time," declares the Lord. "I will put my law in their minds and write it on their hearts. I will be their God, and they will be my people....For I will forgive their wickedness and will remember their sins no more" (Jeremiah 31:33,34b).

However, to the man who does not work but trusts God who justifies the wicked, his faith is credited as righteousness (Romans 4:5).

Talking it over:

1. *Whose work makes the covenant of grace possible?*

2. *Why did the Roman Church in Luther's day teach that salvation is dependent on man's works?*

3. *How did Luther enter into a covenant with God concerning his own soul?*

Section 3

Christ's atonement

Questions to learn:

40. Did our Lord Jesus Christ ever sin?

No. He was holy, blameless, and undefiled.

41. How could the Son of God suffer?

Christ, the Son of God, took flesh and blood, that he might obey and suffer as a man.

42. What is meant by the atonement?

Christ satisfying divine justice, by his sufferings and death, in the place of sinners.

■   ■   ■

Pilate's agreement to crucify Jesus, while releasing the guilty Barabbas, is a picture of Christ's substitutionary suffering for the sins of men. The story is told here from the perspective of Pilate, who probably marvelled at the Jews' choice of a murderer over one so obviously blameless under their God's Law. Until Martin Luther's Ninety-five Theses *were published, the sixteenth-century Roman Church had convinced people that they must help pay for their sins with their own sufferings, especially when the people's sufferings helped the Church.*

The King who died for one, and all

When Pilate left for the Governor's palace around daybreak, his wife was still fast asleep. He knew he would be busy all day keeping the people in line. It was the week of Passover, after all, and Jerusalem was filled with Jews from all over Judea and beyond.

The moment Pilate arrived at the palace he was summoned by some of his guards. As he had feared, a crowd of Jews was already outside clamouring for him. He let them wait for a while to put them in their place, and then went out to meet them.

There on the palace steps were his usual critics—the chief priests, elders and teachers of the Law—angry and demanding. They had brought some poor man with them whom they had bound and beaten.

"We want you to try this man," several of them announced as soon as Pilate appeared in the doorway. "He must be executed."

"Is this Jesus who I've heard so much about?" Pilate asked, already wishing he had not come to the palace that morning. "What charges do you bring against him?"

"He's a criminal," an elder responded vaguely. "We would not be handing him over to you if he were not guilty."

His suspicions now thoroughly aroused, Pilate said, "Take him and try him according to your own law and leave me out of it."

"He must be condemned under Roman law," the elder insisted. "You will not allow us to execute for violations of our law, and so you must try him."

"But what Roman law has he violated?" Pilate asked again.

"Well,…he has stirred up the whole nation," the chief priest announced with a dramatic wave of his arm. "He claims to be a king, the Christ, and…and he opposes paying taxes to Caesar." (This last charge was an outright lie.)

Tired of their wild accusations, Pilate turned his back on them and went inside his palace. He knew that the Jewish leaders were jealous of Jesus because of his wise teachings, miracles and his many followers.

"Bring Jesus to me," he ordered his guards.

They returned with the bound Jesus a few moments later. Nothing about him was threatening, or for that matter very "kingly," thought Pilate.

"Aren't you going to answer their charges?" Pilate asked him. "*Are you the king of the Jews?"*

"*Yes, it is as you say,*" Jesus replied. "But *my kingdom is not of this world. If it were, my servants would fight to prevent my arrest by the Jews. But now my kingdom is from another place.*"

"*You are a king, then!*" Pilate seized on this, still unsure how it was a crime.

"*You are right in saying I am a king. In fact, for this reason I was born, and for this I came into the world, to testify to the truth. Everyone on the side of truth listens to me.*"

"What odd words!" Pilate thought. "I have never heard anyone talk like this. Surely his claims are preposterous!" But he grew a bit nervous.

Just then a servant entered and handed Pilate a note marked, "Urgent!" It was from his wife, and it said: "You will be asked to try an innocent man today. Have nothing to do with him, for I already have suffered greatly in a dream about him this morning."

That was enough for Pilate. He would have Jesus beaten to appease his accusers, and then let him go. He went back out to the leaders, who had by now attracted a curious throng of festival-goers.

"I have examined this man and find no basis for your charges against him," said Pilate. "He has committed no crime deserving death, so I will release him after he has been beaten."

The mob, whom the Jewish leaders had been coaching, jeered angrily at this verdict. They screamed, "Crucify him! Crucify him! Crucify him!" Afraid they would incite the whole town into a riot, Pilate cast about in his mind for another plan.

"Here's what I will do for you," he finally announced. "According to custom, I will free one Jewish prisoner in honour of your Passover. It will either be Jesus, or that murderer Barabbas. The other will be crucified. Which would you have me free?" Surely they would rather have Jesus released to them than a known murderer!

"Barabbas," they said in unison, and without hesitation.

Pilate shook his head and swallowed hard. "Very well, then, let this innocent man's blood be on your heads, not mine! Guards, release Barabbas, and take Jesus to be crucified in his place."

Taken from: Matthew 27:11–26; Luke 23:2; John 18:28–40.

134

From the Bible:

How much more, then, will the blood of Christ, who through the eternal Spirit offered himself unblemished to God, cleanse our consciences from acts that lead to death, so that we may serve the living God! For this reason Christ is the mediator of a new covenant, that those who are called may receive the promised eternal inheritance—now that he has died as a ransom to set them free from the sins committed under the first covenant (Hebrews 9:14–15).

God made him who had no sin to be sin for us, so that in him we might become the righteousness of God (2 Corinthians 5:21).

Talking it over:

1. *Did Jesus submit to Pilate and the Jewish leaders voluntarily?*

2. *In the account, what guilty person was freed because of Jesus' willingness to die? What other guilty persons deserve to suffer instead of Jesus?*

3. *In what sense did Jesus suffer in your place?*

Three florins or one perfect life for your sins?

As quiet as a mouse, William the Baker tiptoed past his village church on the outskirts of Wittenberg, Germany, late one evening in the fall of 1517. He was determined not to disturb Father Luther on this particular evening, for he feared he had drunk one too many an ale to escape his priest's notice.

"On the other hand," William told himself, "I just paid for my sins yesterday." So he kicked a wooden barrel over defiantly, resenting the nagging guilt that plagued him. The barrel rolled across the street and smashed right into the side door of the church.

Out came Martin Luther, working late as usual writing letters, preparing sermons and lectures, and balancing accounts. He rubbed his tired eyes and squinted into the darkness to locate the one responsible for all the commotion. There stood William, swaying back and forth trying not to fall over.

"William? Is that you?" Luther asked. "Are you all right?"

"Aye, Fader Lutter, uh, Luther I mean. I, I, …I'm well."

"What was all that noise?" Luther asked.

"Thanoise?" William thought hard. "Ye! Twas a mighty calamerin', weren't it? Twas that ol' church cat Ebenezer playin' on the barrel thar. Seems he managed to tippy top it over. Yassir, thass what happin'."

William hoped he had paid enough for his indulgence to pardon him also for one little white lie told to his parish priest. He must be careful, though, because his account might be running low at this point.

Luther stepped up to William and sniffed. He drew back, repulsed by the strong odor of liquor. "William! You are drunk! What is the meaning of this?"

William stared back, dumbfounded. No words at all came to mind now, neither truth nor lies. Finally he remembered the piece of paper in the pouch at his side. Relieved, he pulled it out and handed it to the indignant man in front of him. Then he promptly plopped backwards in the dirt, where he sprawled, content.

Luther unfolded the paper. He noticed the official seal of the Holy Roman Church at the top. Then he read aloud:

> This Certificate of Indulgence is issued by His Eminence
> Pope Leo X to William the Baker in acknowledgment of his

contribution of three gold florins for the rebuilding of St. Peter's Basilica in Rome. This contribution demonstrates that William the Baker is duly contrite for all sins he has committed since his baptism, and is deemed adequate penalty for said sins, which are hereby declared forgiven by God. Signed, John Tetzel (representative of Pope Leo X), September 25, 1517.

William looked up at Luther and smiled, hoping the priest would agree that this paper proved that he was contrite enough to make up for tonight's indiscretions, as well as for those he had committed earlier. Friar Tetzel had promised as much, in exchange for one additional florin that William had given him on the sly. But Luther looked unconvinced.

In fact, Luther was furious that Tetzel was across the river tricking his parishioners into paying money that they could not spare, in order to rebuild a church that did not need to be built, by promising to forgive sins that the pope had no power to forgive. He looked down at the mess of a man lying at his feet, and saw anything but a repentant sinner. Rather, he saw a man whose soul was in grave peril because he had no idea where true forgiveness came from, nor any motivation to find out.

Martin Luther plucked William the Baker out of the dirt and helped him home. Later he would have a long talk with him about the only real hope for forgiveness of sins. Luther would have to tell William that he had given the Church his hard-earned money for nothing, because no amount of money could satisfy God's anger over William's sins—not three florins or three million florins.

Tonight, though, Luther returned to his desk to continue the document that would become known throughout the world and down through history as his *Ninety-five Theses*. In it, he would explain why the Church's practice of selling indulgences was a deceit that kept people from understanding that Jesus Christ already has paid the full price for sin. Luther would write of the blasphemy that led sinners to believe that indulgences, rather than the cross of Christ alone, were necessary in order for God to pardon sins. Luther would post his *Ninety-five Theses* on the door of Castle Church in Wittenberg on October 31, 1517, so that it would be noticed and read by other theologians and scholars the following day.

And it certainly was noticed. Luther's actions eventually shook all of Europe to its core. God's reformation of his Church had officially begun.

From the Bible:

For you know that it was not with perishable things such as silver or gold that you were redeemed from the empty way of life handed down to you from your forefathers, but with the precious blood of Christ, a lamb without blemish or defect....Through him you believe in God, who raised him from the dead and glorified him, and so your faith and hope are in God (1 Peter 1:18–19,21).

For Christ died for sins once for all, the righteous for the unrighteous, to bring you to God. He was put to death in the body but made alive by the Spirit (1 Peter 3:18).

Talking it over:

1. *How were people in Luther's time trying to obtain God's forgiveness for their sins? Do you think there is any amount of money that would have sufficiently paid for their sins?*

2. *What is the only thing that atones for our sin?*

3. *Why could Jesus pay for our sin, but we cannot?*

Justification and sanctification

Questions to learn:

43. What did God the Father undertake in the covenant of grace?

To justify and sanctify those for whom Christ should die.

44. What is justification?

It is God regarding sinners as if they had never sinned.

45. What is sanctification?

It is God making sinners holy in heart and conduct.

■ ■ ■

Through Christ, God not only redeems us from our sin, but makes us holy. The brokenhearted woman of Luke 7, who loved Jesus much, must have fully appreciated the miracle of Jesus' justification of sinners. The eighteenth-century pastor and former slave trader John Newton was deeply grateful for the sanctification that he had experienced in his own life throughout the years that he had known the Saviour.

The woman who was forgiven much

A constant stream of villagers filed past the sorrowful woman who shrank back into the shadows outside the home of Simon, the town's leading Pharisee. No one spoke to her, and she spoke to none of them. Though a few looked her way by accident, they quickly turned their heads when they saw who she was.

The woman did not blame them. As usual, she felt dirty. How was she going to get out of this mess she had gotten herself into? Who would ever forgive her for all the evil she had done?

As she fought back tears, the woman clutched the small jar in her hand a little tighter. Soon, another cluster of men approached from the road that led up to Simon's house.

"Do you think he will really come?" one of the men asked another. "Surely Jesus knows that Simon and his crowd will try to prove him a fake."

The woman in the shadows could barely keep from calling out as they passed her by without a glance. "What about his miracles?" she wanted to ask, "and his teachings about love and forgiveness?" Why, rumour had it that Jesus had allowed a tax collector to travel with him! And Jesus treated the man as if his past no longer mattered. Perhaps he would even…well,… No, surely not. Would he? Tonight would tell.

Trembling, the woman pulled her scarf up over her face and stepped out into the light. Somehow no one seemed to notice as she slipped in with the others to hear Jesus.

At first she sat at the back, and watched Jesus recline at the table with Simon and several important guests invited to eat with them. Jesus talked calmly and confidently with the Pharisees, even though the woman was sure they were trying to trick him into saying something wrong, something they could condemn him for. He seemed to have compassion for them in spite of their deceit. Without a thought for herself now, the woman drew closer and closer until she found herself kneeling and crying at Jesus' feet.

Unmindful of the gasps of the host and many of the guests, the woman pulled the small alabaster jar from her smock, uncorked it, and allowed the strong perfume inside to fill the house. When the fragrance reached Jesus, he looked down at her and she saw that he too was near tears. His look said,

"Yes, I know what you are, but still you may touch me."

She poured the perfume on his feet, washed them with her tears and kisses, and wiped them with her hair.

All the while, Simon and his guests exchanged glances. The woman noticed the growing disdain in the way some of them looked at Jesus, and she worried that she might be the very instrument by which they would trap him.

Then Jesus turned to his host and said, *"Simon, I have something to tell you."*

"Tell me, teacher," Simon said, reluctantly.

"Two men owed money to a certain money-lender. One owed him five hundred denarii, and the other fifty. Neither of them had the money to pay him back, so he cancelled the debts of both. Now, which of them will love him more?" Jesus asked.

"I suppose the one who had the bigger debt cancelled," said Simon.

"You have judged correctly," Jesus said, and then pointed down at the sinful woman at his feet.

"Do you see this woman?" He asked Simon, but did not wait for a reply. *"I came into your house. You did not give me any water for my feet, but she wet my feet with her tears and wiped them with her hair.…Therefore, I tell you, her many sins have been forgiven—for she loved much. But he who has been forgiven little loves little."*

Jesus looked back down and said to the woman, *"Your faith has saved you; go in peace."* And for the first time in many, many years, the woman felt clean.

Taken from: Luke 7:36–50.

From the Bible:

This righteousness from God comes through faith in Jesus Christ to all who believe. There is no difference, for all have sinned and fall short of the glory of God, and are justified freely by his grace through the redemption that came by Christ Jesus (Romans 3:22–24).

But God demonstrates his own love for us in this: While we were still sinners, Christ died for us. Since we have now been justified by his blood, how much more shall we be saved from God's wrath through him! (Romans 5:8–9)

Talking it over:

1. *Was Simon any different from the sinful woman in God's eyes? What were the differences between them?*

2. *Even though the woman had sinned greatly, how did she become justified before God?*

3. *Why do you think the woman loved Jesus more than Simon did?*

God's amazing grace

"William, my boy, come right in, come right in," John Newton beckoned to the young man waiting outside his study at London's St. Mary Woolnoth Church.

William Wilberforce was quite happy to "come right in," as he was eager to escape the more public areas of the church where he might be seen by one of his fellow parliamentarians. He was not sure he wanted them to think he was keeping company with evangelical Christians, a much reviled group in 1785.

"I was delighted to hear that you wanted an appointment with me, son," said the sixty-year-old vicar. "Now what can I do for you?"

"Well, sir, …I, I've had a rather strange thing happen to me lately, and I don't know quite what to do about it," William began.

John was intrigued. He had learned over the years that when someone spoke of "something strange" with the surprised but thrilled anticipation that he had just heard in William's voice, it always seemed to have something to do with God.

"And?" John coaxed. "Tell me. What has God done?"

"I guess the best way to say it, sir, is that I have realized that Christ Jesus died to save me."

"Ah, excellent!" John said, clapping William on the back. "So you finally see. I have prayed for this for a long time. But you are concerned by it?"

"It's just that…well, you know that I was elected to Parliament a few years back, and I…I love the work. I just don't know that I'm ready to quit and become a preacher." There, he'd said it.

John resisted the urge to laugh. Clearly, the young man was quite serious about his dilemma. "William, one thing you will discover is that God can use us anywhere. We can't always know how he intends to fit us into his plan. He often has to do a lot of work in us before he can use us anyway. Let me tell you a story.

"When I was a young man roughly your age, I was a slave trader. I was captain of a ship that I sailed to Africa, where we bought people who had been kidnapped from their homes, and then took them to America and sold them for a huge profit.

"This was actually a step up for me, as I had spent the ten years before doing as much damage to myself and God's name as he would graciously permit. For you see, God knew he would eventually get my attention, and so in his infinite mercy he tolerated my endless blasphemies and crimes and even suicidal despair. I believe he saved my life many times over; and finally he saved my soul too.

"But, I was still just a babe in Christ. For years after I first believed in him, I ran that slave ship. Perhaps the conditions on my ship were better than most, but we still kept our captives bound like cattle in the hold of the ship for weeks, and then sold them like so much meat in the marketplace of human corruption.

"Over time, God showed me that the slave trade, which the world had come to accept as necessary and thus righteous enough, was in fact abhorrent to my Lord. Slowly, he made it abhorrent to me as well. Nevertheless, God himself had to deliver me from the profession. In my twenty-ninth year, a few days before I was to set sail on my fourth voyage as captain, I suffered a mild stroke and was unable to go. The captain who took my place lost his life on board that ship, and I never went to sea again.

"The Lord provided me with a job on land. In addition, as I studied his word, he instilled in me a passion to preach of Christ. I realized I was especially fit to tell people all that the Lord can do because of all he'd had to do in me. It pleased him, however, to wait several years before giving me a church in which to preach. Though I often felt frustrated about my situation, I see now how he increased my knowledge and love for him as a result of those circumstances.

"That was over twenty years ago. You can see that my heart has grown much since I first believed. In just the past few years, for example, he has given me a passion to see my former profession abolished. His grace is truly amazing!

"All this is to say, William, that you must grow in Christ wherever you are. And if he has led you to Parliament, you may be assured that he means to use you there. In fact, he can use you more and more there as your heart becomes more holy. Perhaps as he purifies your heart he will use you in your post to abolish such evils as the slave trade itself."

William Wilberforce left St. Mary Woolnoth Church with his head held higher and his tender heart free of worry. He became one of England's most respected statesmen, known by all as a devout evangelical Christian. Before his death in 1833, he had pushed through Parliament the laws necessary to forever abolish the sale of slaves. Like John Newton before him, William learned all about the amazing grace of Christ Jesus, by which God brings men to himself and makes them holy in heart and deed.

From the Bible:

> May God himself, the God of peace, sanctify you through and through. May your whole spirit, soul and body be kept blameless at the coming of our Lord Jesus Christ. The one who calls you is faithful and he will do it (1 Thessalonians 5:23–24).

> [W]e have not stopped praying for you and asking God to fill you with the knowledge of his will through all spiritual wisdom and understanding. And we pray this in order that you may live a life worthy of the Lord and may please him in every way: bearing fruit in every good work, growing in the knowledge of God, being strengthened with all power according to his glorious might so that you may have great endurance and patience (Colossians 1:9b–11).

Talking it over:

1. *What is sanctification? When does it take place? How long does it take?*

2. *Tell some of the ways God sanctified John Newton.*

3. *How do you think God is working to sanctify you right now (if you are a Christian)? Are you fully cooperating with him?*

Christ obeyed and suffered

Questions to learn:

46. For whom did Christ obey and suffer?

For those whom the Father had given him.

47. What kind of life did Christ live on earth?

A life of perfect obedience to the Law of God.

48. What kind of death did Christ die?

The painful and shameful death of the cross.

■ ■ ■

In the garden of Gethsemane, Jesus poured out to his Father the sorrow with which he faced his final act of obedience—dying on a cross. The early church historian Eusebius records the story of Agbarus, a ruler in the time of Jesus who asked the Lord to come to his kingdom and heal him. But Jesus would not be deterred from the ultimate purpose for which he had come to earth —to be crucified and resurrected.

The cup of Christ's suffering

James could not recall ever being so confused before. His beloved Jesus had spent the evening warning the disciples that one of them would soon betray him, and that the rest of them would fall away! Even worse, Jesus kept talking about suffering, about leaving them, and about "pouring out his blood." Everything seemed calm enough, but Jesus always knew things that James did not.

James closely watched his Lord, who walked a few steps ahead of the disciples. He tried to convince himself that nothing would happen to Jesus so long as he kept his eye on him. Jesus seemed to be headed for the garden at the foot of the Mount of Olives, where he often prayed when he was in Jerusalem.

Peter and John trudged along next to James. When he stole a glance at them, they stared back with the same wonder and apprehension that shrouded his own heart. No one said anything; there was nothing to say.

Soon they were in a small clearing among the olive trees in the garden of Gethsemane. There, Jesus stopped abruptly and turned to them. His face was streaked with tears, his forehead creased in grief. He stood with one hand against his chest. "*My soul is overwhelmed with sorrow to the point of death*," he told them.

James wanted to rush forward and comfort his Lord, but the anguish of Jesus was too great. James could not get any nearer to it.

"*Stay here and keep watch*," Jesus said to them. "*Pray that you will not fall into temptation.*" Then he walked several yards away and fell to the ground.

"Yes, I should do that. I should pray," James thought. "But, why is my Lord so troubled? What is going to happen to him? I can't bear it if he goes away. What will we do if he does?" Overcome by these fears, James felt his eyes grow heavy. He laid down on the ground, and the fear receded into the darkness as he gave himself over to sleep. The others did likewise.

A stone's throw away, Jesus poured out his sorrow to the Father. "*Father,*" he said, "*everything is possible for you. If you are willing, take this cup from me.*" The cup he spoke of was his upcoming, agonizing death on the cross. He knew he would have to take the sin of the whole world onto himself in order to pay the penalty for it on the cross. He—who had never sinned—would

have to become sin so that those who believed in him could be forgiven and have everlasting life.

He knew too that the Father could not allow sin into his holy presence. Then, while Jesus hung on the cross, weighed down by all the world's ugliness, the Father would strike him, crush him and forsake him. This was the suffering he really dreaded. This was the payment, the atonement, the horror of God's wrath. The unspeakable physical pain and earthly humiliation that awaited Jesus on the cross were secondary.

Drops of sweat that were like blood formed on his brow as he prayed.

"Yet not my will, but yours be done," Jesus cried out in love and obedience to the Father who had sent him for this very purpose.

James, had he been awake at that moment, would have seen a golden lightbeam from heaven touch down in the grass next to his kneeling Lord. He might have discerned that the lightbeam was actually an angel of God, whose appearance strengthened Jesus.

This cup of suffering *was* the Father's will. By it he would make a way for his human children to come to him. In his heart, Jesus took the cup and began to drink.

He thanked the Father, rose, and returned to the sleeping disciples. James felt a nudge, and heard Jesus say, *"Could you not keep watch for one hour? The spirit is willing, but the body is weak."*

"Rise! Let us go! Here is my betrayer!" Jesus said, as Judas led a crowd into the clearing, walked up to Jesus, and kissed him.

Taken from: Matthew 26:36–49; Mark 14:32–45; Luke 22:39–48.

From the Bible:

"I am saying nothing beyond what the prophets and Moses said would happen—that the Christ would suffer and, as the first to rise from the dead, would proclaim light to his own people and to the Gentiles" (Acts 26:22b–23).

"Father, the time has come. Glorify your Son, that your Son may glorify you. For you granted him authority over all people that he might give eternal life to all those you have given him" (John 17:1b–2).

Talking it over:

1. *What was the difference between how Jesus handled his sorrow, and how James, Peter and John did? What does this show about Jesus?*

2. *Did Jesus dread dying on the cross? Why did he dread it most?*

3. *Did Jesus willingly die on the cross for our sins?*

4. *Imagine for a moment all the evil things that everyone has ever done being on the heart of one person. Does it make you love Jesus more that he was willing to do this for us?*

Life from death

Several men-in-waiting huddled around King Agbarus' bed and fretted over him. One touched his forehead. Was it too hot? Was it too cold? Who could tell?

Agbarus brushed the doting hand aside impatiently. He had his own plan.

"Bring Ananias to me at once!" he commanded, and watched one of his attendants scurry off to find the courier. Moments later, Ananias entered and approached the king's bed.

"I wish to dictate a letter to Jesus of Nazareth, the Jew who has been performing miracles in Judea. I will ask him to come and heal me," Agbarus announced. "Write this down:

> I, Agbarus, Prince of Edessa, the great nation beyond the Euphrates, send greetings to Jesus, whose righteousness and miracles I have heard many reports of. They say that without medicines or herbs you cleanse lepers, give sight to the blind and strength to the lame, cast out demons and raise the dead. Many also say that you have lived a perfectly innocent life, always doing only good. After much consideration of these things, I have concluded that you are either God or are the son of God. I therefore beseech you to come and heal me of the disease from which I have suffered for many years, as none here know what to do for me. If you come you may stay. For I have heard that the other Jews are jealous and are plotting against you. Please note that Edessa is a modest but excellent kingdom, sufficient for us both.

As he finished his dictation, many in the circle around the king's bed gasped. Surely this was the futile act of a desperate man!

"Sire, you are offering to share your kingdom with him?" whispered an old man who had attended Agbarus from the time he was a small boy.

"Yes, Beram. If this conclusion that has come to me is correct, I should be grateful if he would let *me* stay. Now off with you Ananias. I grow weary."

Several weeks later, Beram entered Agbarus' bedchamber while he was

resting. "Sire," he said, shaking the king. "Ananias has returned. Enter, Ananias."

"Is Jesus with you?" Agbarus asked the courier eagerly.

"No, Sire, but he sent this message back to you: 'You are blessed, Agbarus, for, without seeing, you have believed in me! It is written about me that some who see will not believe, whereas others who do not see will nevertheless believe and live. However, I cannot come to you now. Instead, I must soon fulfill all things for which I came. After I return to him who sent me, one of my disciples will come to heal your body and give you and yours eternal life!'"

Agbarus, who had been straining forward during the reading of Jesus' letter, fell back into his pillow. He promised himself that he would not die until Jesus' man came.

Soon word arrived in Edessa that Jesus had been crucified. Still, Agbarus hoped.

And there came a day, many months later, when Agbarus heard talk of a stranger in Edessa named Thaddeus who was healing every kind of ailment in the name of Jesus Christ. Suspecting that he might be Jesus' promised disciple, the king summoned him. For the occasion, Agbarus assembled all his nobles in the great hall of his palace. When Thaddeus entered, Agbarus saw a light shining down from heaven onto the face of Thaddeus, and to the amazement of his nobles who saw no light, Agbarus fell on his knees before the stranger. "Are you really Jesus' disciple?" Agbarus asked.

"Because you have great confidence in the Lord Jesus, he has sent me to you," Thaddeus assured him. "And as your faith grows, he will enable you to live in obedience to his commands and to enjoy abundant life."

"How I wish he had come when I wrote to him," Agbarus said. "I would have defended him against the Jews."

"By submitting to crucifixion, sire, the Lord Jesus fulfilled his Father's will, and having done so, was resurrected and taken up to him again," said Thaddeus. "For the sake of those whom the Father has given him, Jesus had to be crucified, and nothing could have kept him from it."

"I believe in him and in his Father," Agbarus said.

Thaddeus placed his hand on the head of Agbarus. "I have been given authority to heal your illness in the name of Christ Jesus," he said, and Agbarus felt new strength pour into his body and soul.

"Please tell me more about Jesus," he implored Thaddeus.

"I will not tell you alone," Thaddeus answered, "for I have been sent to bring this news to one and all. Therefore you must assemble the people of your kingdom tomorrow, and I will tell you everything I know about Jesus. I will sow among you and your people the word of life that springs from the death of Jesus." And this he did.

From the Bible:

Who has believed our message and to whom has the arm of the Lord been revealed? …[H]e was pierced for our transgressions, he was crushed for our iniquities; the punishment that brought us peace was upon him, and by his wounds we are healed.…Yet it was the Lord's will to crush him and cause him to suffer.…Therefore I will give him a portion among the great, …because he poured out his life unto death, and was numbered with the transgressors (Isaiah 53:1,5,10a,12a,c).

And being found in appearance as a man, he humbled himself and became obedient to death—even death on a cross! (Philippians 2:8)

Talking it over:

1. *What are all the ways that Jesus was obedient to his Father?*

2. *Why did Jesus suffer and die on the cross? Could anything have deterred him from that purpose?*

3. *The verse above, from the book of Isaiah, was recorded by one of God's prophets hundreds of years before Jesus lived. Do you think it had always been God's will that Jesus would be crucified?*

UNIT 4

OUR RESPONSE TO THE GOSPEL

Repentance and belief

Questions to learn:

49. Who will be saved?

Only those who repent of sin and believe in Christ.

50. What is it to repent?

To be sorry for sin, and to hate and forsake it because it is displeasing to God.

51. What is it to believe in Christ?

To trust in Christ alone for salvation.

■   ■   ■

When an earthquake shook the Philippi jail in which Paul and Silas were imprisoned, God used them to bring the frightened Philippian jailer to an earnest trust in Christ. As a teenage boy, the nineteenth-century pastor Charles Spurgeon had long hated and grieved over his youthful sins. After much fruitless searching for relief from this guilt, he was given forgiveness and faith through the simple gospel message—"Look to Christ."

The earthquake and the jailer's broken heart

On most days the jailer could tolerate his job as the head warden of the Roman prison in Philippi. After all, he had a family to feed, and the pay was good. One always could make more doing a job that no one else wanted to do.

Today had not been such a great one, though. The prison was already overcrowded, and then they had brought him those Christians—Silas and Paul.

As the two severely beaten men were dragged in unconscious, the magistrate had warned the jailer dramatically, "These men are troublemakers; their teaching has provoked riots throughout the city. Watch them carefully."

Wondering how two such battered men could cause any more trouble, the jailer nevertheless obediently had them taken to the centre of the prison and locked into the most secure cell. And, though they were still unconscious, he had their feet shackled, just to be safe. "I hope no one makes me torture them further," he thought.

The jailer decided he had better stick close by since he had been given such strict orders. So he sent the other guards home and settled down for a long night. Soon he was asleep in the outer room.

Some hours later, Paul and Silas awoke, and began to sing praises to God. The other prisoners who had seen the pair brought in near death a few hours earlier could not believe their ears. Such melodies had never been heard in these cells before. They listened, quiet and thoughtful.

At midnight, the jail began to tremble. Plaster crumbled from the ceiling in the inner cell, dropping onto Paul and Silas as they began another hymn. Soon, the shaking grew more violent. The prisoners' chains came loose and their prison doors fell open.

The sleeping jailer awoke when he heard iron clanging against iron. Disoriented, he wondered where he was. Then came the horrible moment when he saw that the cell doors stood wide open and he recalled how heavily the prisoners outnumbered him. If they had not already escaped through the back door, they would easily overpower him now.

"This will cost me my life," he thought. The rule for operating prisons was a simple one: if a criminal escaped, the careless guard responsible for it would pay for the crime in his place.

164

"But," the fearful jailer thought, "I will not put my family through a disgraceful trial. I will carry out the sentence on myself." Pulling the sword from his belt, he pointed it at his own chest and was just about to thrust when a shout came from within the inner cell.

"*Don't harm yourself! We are all here!*" Paul called out. Thinking himself delirious, the jailer lit a lamp, looked in, and found that his prisoners were indeed all still there, though not one of them remained chained.

He fell trembling at Paul and Silas' feet, his shocked mind vividly recounting all the things he had heard about these men and their master, Jesus Christ. They said Jesus was the Son of God and forgave sins. Should he have listened more closely to their message? Instead he had unwittingly taken part in a Roman quarrel against God. How could he have helped to persecute them so, shackling them when they were too weak to stand up? Yet here they stood, beaming at him amidst the rubble of a jail that could no longer hold them!

In the face of Silas and Paul's joy and faith, the Philippian jailer was acutely aware of the eternal need in his soul. He thought about how long he had pursued his own selfish course. Where was it leading him? Though he now saw what a sudden, certain thing death was, he had never before considered what lay beyond it. He asked desperately, "*Sirs, what must I do to be saved?*"

"*Believe in the Lord Jesus, and you will be saved*, my friend," Paul answered him. And the Philippian jailer did believe.

Then he took Paul and Silas back to his home, washed their wounds, and woke his household. They listened to Paul explain the whole truth about Jesus, and every one of them repented and believed in him. That very night, Paul and Silas baptized them.

At daybreak, the rejoicing jailer received an unexpected order from the magistrate to release the apostles. "Why, it is almost as if they were sent to my jail just for me," he thought joyfully. "Imagine all the suffering on my behalf. How much God loved me, even when I ignored my sin and persecuted my Saviour!"

Taken from: Acts 16:16–36.

From the Bible:

"For God so loved the world that he gave his one and only Son, that whoever believes in him shall not perish but have eternal life. For God did not send his Son into the world to condemn the world, but to save the world through him" (John 3:16–17).

Or do you show contempt for the riches of his kindness, tolerance and patience, not realizing that God's kindness leads you toward repentance? (Romans 2:4)

Talking it over:

1. *One way God leads us to repent is to show us his holiness and power so that we can see how sinful and weak we are in comparison to him. How did God show the jailer his holiness and power? How did the jailer feel about God and himself as a result?*

2. *Another way God leads us to repent is to show us his mercy and love so that we turn away from our sin and seek to please him. How did God show the jailer his mercy and love?*

3. *When the Philippian jailer asked Paul and Silas how he could be saved, what one thing did they tell him?*

4. *Can we be saved from our sins by believing in anything else but Jesus, or by doing anything else besides believing in him? Why not?*

"Look unto me"

Fifteen-year-old Charles Haddon Spurgeon descended the back stairs at the Newmarket school where he was both pupil and underteacher for the younger students. He tried to put something of a spring in his step so that anyone he might meet up with besides old Mary the cook would not see his misery. When he entered the kitchen, Charles found Mary alone in the pantry sorting potatoes.

At once Mary detected the boy's torment. She had seen it on his face before, and had lately spent much time on her knees on his behalf. "Charlie, sit yourself down and tell me your trouble, son," she commanded, snatching a stool out of nowhere and plopping it down next to a large pile of potatoes.

With a heavy sigh, Charles sat down. When he thought he could speak without crying, he told her, "Mary, I...I, I'm afraid God is going to send me to hell!" There, he'd said it, but didn't seem to feel any better having done so.

"All right, Charlie. What makes you think this?" she asked, patting his arm.

"Because I can't stop, I just can't stop sinning, Mary, no matter how I promise to and set my mind against all the things I know God hates. Why, I can't even tell you what I was thinking just last night. It took me until this morning to stop thinking those thoughts, and still they are just under the surface ready to rise up in my mind again. I can feel it, Mary. I won't be able to keep them out for long.

"Don't you see what this means?" he continued. "God wouldn't be righteous if he would tolerate such things from me! And I know he won't, Mary. God *is* righteous, and he is just. He should send me to hell. But I can't bear it. What am I going to do?"

"Charlie, I can tell you that the way to God for all of us is through Jesus Christ. He's the one who paid for your sins, and he's coming for you, son. I believe that. I've been asking God for that, and you need to as well. Now go. I must have breakfast on the table shortly!"

When Charles went home to Colchester for Christmas break a few days later, he still didn't really understand what Mary had told him. He had certainly been asking God for mercy, but he simply couldn't believe that a just God would forgive the wretchedness he saw in his own heart. He could think of nothing that he could possibly do to persuade God to forgive him for all this!

Each Sunday during the break, Charles roused himself out of the despair that threatened to overwhelm him, and went to church hoping that in one of the sermons he would hear what his heart so longed to know—what did he need to do to have his sins forgiven? But each Sunday he was disappointed by sermons that seemed to answer every question but the one he asked.

On Sunday, January 6, 1850, Charles awoke while it was still dark. Outside, snow fell heavily onto Colchester and the surrounding countryside. Inside, his heart fell further into hopeless sorrow even as he searched his Bible and prayed for the answer to his question.

Later that morning, Charles set out for a church his parents had told him about. But God had a different plan. A snow drift blocked his path and diverted him into another church—a tiny Primitive Methodist chapel down a nearby side street. Only a dozen or so others had made it through the storm that morning, but the preacher was not among them. As Charles joined the small group, a very simple-looking fellow, probably a shoemaker or tailor, slid out of his pew and stepped up to the pulpit.

"The text this mornin' is 'Look unto me, and be ye saved.' Isaiah 45:22," he managed to stammer out, barely able to read. "My dear friends, this is a very simple text. It says, 'Look.' You see, *anybody* can look. You don't need a college education to look. It's not hard work. You don't have to lift your hand or even your finger to look. Why, a fool can do it. A child can do it. A poor man or a rich one. Just 'look.'

"But look at what? It says here, 'Look unto *me*.' That is Christ. Don't look to yourself and say, 'What can *I* do?', but look unto *Christ*. Don't look to God the Father and say, 'Am I one of your chosen ones?' Just look at *Christ*. Jesus says, 'Look unto me; I'm hanging on a cross for you, sweatin' great drops of blood. Look unto me; I'm dead and buried, and rise again, for you. Look unto *me*, where I've risen to sit at the Father's right hand and plead for him to see you through my blood. Oh sinner, look unto *me*.'"

About that time, the self-styled preacher pointed at Charles and said, "Young man, you seem altogether miserable. And you always will be until you obey this text. You have nothin' to do but look. Look at Jesus Christ and live."[7]

Charles heard nothing else the man said. His eyes left his own dejected self, and found Jesus in all his glory. "Of course," he thought, "here is God's mercy, his forgiveness, and his justice. This is the way to salvation. It's not me; it's all in him."

When Charles returned home, his family saw that the cloud had been lifted. "Tell us what wonderful thing has happened to you," his mother encouraged.

Charles Spurgeon never stopped telling the people of England about the marvellous Saviour who cleanses us from our wretched sin when we look at him and believe. Spurgeon became one of the most influential ministers of the nineteenth century, respected for his passionate faithfulness to God's Word in an age when many others had grown complacent and worldly in their attitudes toward the Lord.

From the Bible:

[Y]et now I am happy, not because you were made sorry, but because your sorrow led you to repentance. For you became sorrowful as God intended....Godly sorrow brings repentance that leads to salvation and leaves no regret, but worldly sorrow brings death (2 Corinthians 7:9a,10).

The Lord said to Moses, "Make a snake and put it up on a pole; anyone who is bitten can look at it and live" (Numbers 21:8).

Just as Moses lifted up the snake in the desert, so the Son of Man must be lifted up, that everyone who believes in him may have eternal life (John 3:14–15).

Talking it over:

1. *From the story, how do you know that Charles Spurgeon repented of his sins?*

2. *Repentance alone is not enough to be saved from our sin. What else is needed?*

3. *How did God lead Charles Spurgeon to believe in Jesus Christ for his salvation?*

The Holy Spirit

Questions to learn:

52. Can you repent and believe in Christ by your own power?

No. I can do nothing good without God's Holy Spirit.

53. How can you receive the Holy Spirit?

God has told us that we must pray to him for the Holy Spirit.

■   ■   ■

God's Holy Spirit enables us to repent and believe. The Holy Spirit led Paul to Philippi to proclaim the truth about Christ to Lydia and her household, and thereafter opened Lydia's heart to understand her need for a Saviour. Over the years, however, many overzealous preachers have not trusted in God's Spirit to accomplish a genuine, inward work of grace in people's lives. One such man was the famous nineteenth-century revivalist Charles Finney, whose preaching often worked people into an emotional fervour that they sadly mistook for salvation.

The opened heart

Claudius admired the selection of sheer linens that his supplier had spread across the floor of his gift stall in the Philippi marketplace. "Lydia, you must have every colour imaginable, but my favourite is still the 'royal purple.' And it's my best seller too. The wealthy Roman officials are especially fond of it."

Lydia accepted Claudius' compliment with a smile. She imported the "royal purple" from her business contacts back in Thyatira, and had already noticed how much it was in demand among the many Roman soldiers and dignitaries who were now living in Philippi. She had certainly made her move to this bustling town at just the right moment, financially speaking.

But money had not really been her motive. She still was not quite sure why she had decided to uproot her household and move to a new province. After all, it was especially hard for her to practice her religion here, because there were so few Jews in Philippi. They didn't even have a synagogue in which to meet. She herself was not a Jew, but she had come to see that the God of the Jewish Scriptures was the only true God. Somehow she felt that he had drawn her here, that he was trying to show her something she had been unable to see before.

Ten miles east, in the coastal town of Neapolis, Paul was just getting off the ship from Troas. He and his companions—Silas, Luke and Timothy—were on a mission trip from Antioch.

Before sailing, the group had tried to go into two other provinces, but the Holy Spirit had shut the door on those attempts. Then Paul had had a dream about a man from Macedonia, the province that included Philippi. In the dream the man had begged Paul to come and help the Macedonians. So Paul and his companions had travelled from Troas to Neapolis and the door was open wide. They had only to seek out those whose hearts the Holy Spirit was opening to Christ.

The missionaries made their way first to Philippi, arriving just before the Sabbath. Early in the morning of their day of worship, they left the city through the west gate and made their way to the Gangites River, where they had planned to find a quiet place to pray.

Lydia, too, headed toward the river at the first signs of dawn. She had all the women of her household in tow—the personal servants, the weavers and

those who cleaned and dyed the fabrics. They would join the group of God-fearing worshippers at the Gangites.

The women were already in prayer at the riverbank when Paul's group arrived. Seeing them, Paul urgently felt their need for Jesus.

"Have any of you heard about Jesus of Nazareth, the one who was crucified in Jerusalem and on the third day was resurrected to eternal life?" he began.

At the mention of the name, Lydia's heart beat a little faster. "We heard talk of him before we moved here from Thyatira," she admitted. "Who was he?"

"He is the one who sent me to you," Paul said. "His Holy Spirit led me to come to Macedonia and find those whose hearts the Lord was preparing to receive salvation. Before he was crucified, Jesus promised to send his Spirit to reveal the truth about himself to those who would recognize him as their Saviour."

As Paul spoke, that same Spirit of God opened Lydia's heart to all that Paul said so that she understood and joyfully embraced the good news about Christ. This was what she had been yearning for. The women of her household also believed, and all were baptized there on the banks of the Gangites by the four missionaries.

From that moment on, Lydia supported Paul's Macedonian ministry in whatever way she could. She no longer considered herself her own, but put her home and wealth at God's disposal with great thankfulness for the work he had done in her heart.

Taken from: Acts 16:6–15.

From the Bible:

One of those listening was a woman named Lydia, a dealer in purple cloth from the city of Thyatira, who was a worshipper of God. The Lord opened her heart to respond to Paul's message (Acts 16:14).

"If you then, though you are evil, know how to give good gifts to your children, how much more will your Father in heaven give the Holy Spirit to those who ask him!" (Luke 11:13)

Talking it over:

1. *Who was responsible for Lydia's belief in Jesus Christ as her Saviour?*

2. *What were some of the many ways that the Holy Spirit acted in her life and Paul's to bring this about?*

3. *What does Luke 11:13 say about God's desire to give his Holy Spirit to those who ask him for it?*

4. *Was it only for Lydia that the Holy Spirit gave her the gift of faith? After God gives us faith, how might he use us to encourage faith in others?*

The man who tried to save Evans Mills

One evening late in the spring of 1824, a sizable crowd filled the schoolhouse in Evans Mills, New York. Tonight Charles Grandison Finney would light a revivalist fire that would blaze across the American frontier.

But that night, Finney was not happy with what went on. As he warmed to his preaching—explaining yet again about God's judgment and about salvation through Christ—Finney observed his audience. One man in the third row was dozing while his wife smiled and nodded her head now and then at what Finney said. The others also looked pleased with his sermon, when they weren't whispering back and forth making plans for Sunday dinner.

"Why, I've been preaching to them nearly every night for weeks, and they are still staring at me with the same glazed-over serenity. They just don't get it," Finney thought. "I believe it's time to light a fire under their carefree hides."

He stopped mid-sentence and glared at his congregation for a long moment. The woman in the third row nudged her husband awake. Then Finney shouted loudly, "Do you admit that what I've been preaching is the truth? Well, do you?"

Rows of sinners gazed back at him, speechless.

"Most or all of you profess to believe it. But do you really? Know that if you do not repent and believe this moment, then you are rejecting the Lord's gospel. Who is ready to do what he ought to do? A horse may trample you to death tonight and you may never get another chance. Now what will it be?" He raised his voice even louder, and reached far over the lectern pointing his finger around the room. "Those of you who are ready right now to commit to God, stand up. Those of you who wish Christ to understand that you reject him, just sit there."

For what seemed like many minutes, not a head was turned nor a breath exhaled. But all eyes discretely flitted around the room to see what the others would do. No one moved an inch.

"Very well," Finney declared, "you have made your choice! You have rejected the Saviour. Now go home. I will only preach one more night here and then I'll move on to a town where people are willing to turn from their sins and follow Christ. I just hope you are all able to come back here tomorrow night." Then Finney watched silently as the congregation, stunned and bewildered, filed out of the schoolhouse.

The next night, Finney tells us in his memoirs, the anxious townspeople followed him through the streets and packed the schoolhouse "to its utmost capacity." Would this really be their last chance to repent? Who would do it? No one wanted to miss out on the hubbub. Some didn't want to miss out on salvation. Almost everyone was there.

That night, Finney told the people of Evans Mills everything he knew about hell. He preached for more than an hour, describing in great detail the misery of eternity apart from God. By the end of his sermon, the children were weeping into their mothers' laps, all the men were pale, and some of the women were nearly fainting away at the prospect of what lay before them. Just as Finney had planned, the congregation was now a powder keg of emotions.

Finney looked down on them fiercely. "I'll be right here tomorrow night," he said, and abruptly walked out of the schoolhouse. He had given them no chance to repent! The stage was set.

Over the next several nights, the people poured into the schoolhouse in a state of high agitation. Those of every religious and moral persuasion squeezed in. One man brought his gun and threatened to kill Finney for working his wife up into a fervour. Finney took no notice, but preached his heart out and commanded them, "Now, sinners, do your duty and repent of your transgressions. It will be told tonight in heaven and hell what you decide to do. Here is the window you can jump through to salvation. It's open just a bit. Come to the front right now if you choose the way of Christ!"

Revival had come to Evans Mills. Or so it seemed.

As Finney honed his revival style, the people of Evans Mills and nearby towns in which he preached were powerfully moved. On many nights, as he threatened and shamed them, dozens leapt up and made their way to the front. Some came groaning and yelling. Some got only a few steps before they fell to the ground weeping or bawling. Others joined the fray not wanting to be left behind, struggling to the front just to see what would happen. In the end Finney was quite satisfied that the people in and around Evans Mills had come to their senses and grabbed hold of salvation.

Although few doubted that Charles Finney knew the Lord himself, many in his day and since have condemned his methods. He preached as if people could repent of their sins and believe in Christ in their own power, simply by deciding to. It was true that some genuinely came to Christ during these services, but many who thought that they had been converted during Finney's revival meetings had only had their feelings stirred up. Lacking the Holy Spirit's conviction, they were not truly sorry for their sins and did not really trust in Christ. They went forward only because their emotions were inflamed—they feared hell or they thought they wouldn't get another chance. Some went forward just because everyone else did. Sadly, a number of them never recovered from the confusion and disappointment of their "revival" experiences.

From the Bible:

We have not received the spirit of the world but the Spirit who is from God, that we may understand what God has freely given us" (1 Corinthians 2:12).

"Not everyone who says to me, 'Lord, Lord' will enter the kingdom of heaven, but only he who does the will of my Father who is in heaven. Many will say to me on that day, 'Lord, Lord, did we not prophesy in your name, and in your name drive out demons and perform many miracles?' Then I will tell them plainly, 'I never knew you. Away from me, you evildoers!'" (Matthew 7:21–23)

Talking it over:

1. *Remember that repentance means being sorry for sin and forsaking it because it displeases God. Do you think all of the people who came forward in Charles Finney's revival in Evans Mills really became Christians? Why?*

2. *Who does God give us to help us repent of sin and believe in Christ for forgiveness? Can we repent and believe without the Holy Spirit's help?*

3. *Do you think there are people who appear to believe in Christ when they really don't? How do you know if you are truly a Christian? (A true Christian will want to do God's will, and will have some evidence of the Holy Spirit in his life. See Matthew 7.)*

Those before the coming of Christ

Questions to learn:

54. How were godly persons saved before the coming of Christ?

By believing in the Saviour to come.

55. How did they show their faith?

By offering sacrifices on God's altar.

56. What did these sacrifices represent?

Christ, the Lamb of God, who was to die for sinners.

■　■　■

After God had allowed the Jews to be exiled in Babylon for many years, he brought a remnant back to Judea to reconstruct his temple and reinstitute the sacrifices that the Law required. Obedient Jews such as Zerubbabel, who led the remnant back, surely longed for the Messiah whom God's prophets had promised would redeem them from their sins once and for all. Centuries later, the Maccabees reclaimed the temple from Greek invaders who had desecrated it. Their zeal for the sacrificial system was rooted in their faith that God would forgive their sins.

The greatest day

The streets surrounding Jerusalem's glistening new temple were thick with Jews who had returned from the Babylonian exile. They and their families were joined by many non-Jewish Persians—curiosity seekers who wondered what all the commotion was about. Zerubbabel, the Jewish leader who was a descendant of King David, strolled among the merrymakers enjoying the greatest day of his life.

As he dodged a group of musicians dancing across the temple yard, Zerubbabel remembered back to when this adventure had begun—23 years ago when the Lord had moved the heart of King Cyrus to send some of the exiled Jews home to rebuild Solomon's temple. Zerubbabel, a strapping young man then, had awakened one morning to find that God had given him a passion to lead the returning remnant.

The first great day of Zerubbabel's life was the day they had arrived in Jerusalem—all 50,000 of them with their livestock and household goods, as well as with the sacred temple furnishings that Nebuchadnezzar had stolen when he had destroyed the temple a generation before. Later that year, they had completed the rebuilding of the temple altar and had made the first animal sacrifices to the Lord since the Babylonians had taken them captive years ago. How grateful Zerubbabel had been for the opportunity to once again obey God's command to shed the blood of unblemished animals in atonement for the people's many grievous violations of his laws!

Not long after that, he and Jeshua, the high priest, had directed the people to lay the foundation for the new temple. The Lord had blessed this work, and they had held a huge celebration on the day of its completion. Zerubbabel, waving now at old Jeshua on the platform, remembered how the priest had paraded across the temple foundation dressed in his bright vestments, blasting a trumpet in praise to God. Oh, how the people had shouted and sung to the Lord on that day!

Following this celebration, however, the good days had been rarer. The Persians, who were afraid of the Jewish God, had begun to harass Zerubbabel, Jeshua and the temple workers. And the Jews, rather than trusting God to provide a way for them to do what he had commanded, had given up building the temple and instead set to work enlarging their own

homes and planting their fields. The foundation of the Lord's temple had lain bare for sixteen bleak years.

Then one day, a voice had roused the people from their apathy, shouting: "'Leave your plush homes and build my house, *so that I may take pleasure in it and be honoured,*' commands the Lord your God." The voice was that of God's prophet Haggai. When they heard it, Zerubbabel and the people repented of their fear and selfishness, and began to build. Through Haggai, and his fellow prophet Zechariah, God had encouraged them all along the way: "'*Be strong, Oh Zerubbabel. Be strong, Oh Jeshua.* Be strong, all you my people, *and work. For I am with you,*' declares the Lord. '*My Spirit remains among you. Do not fear.*'"

And the Lord's Spirit had guided them and protected their work on his house. Zerubbabel had especially relished the day that their pagan governor had written to the new Persian king, Darius, whining about their progress on the temple. Darius, though, wrote back ordering the governor not to interfere with the rebuilding, but instead to pay the building expenses out of the royal treasury!

Today, towering before Zerubbabel, was their finished work. He had lived to see God fulfill his promises to them. In his joy, Zerubbabel leapt onto the platform and quieted the people. He raised his hands and prayed, "Oh, righteous and almighty God, who delivered our forefathers out of captivity, who disciplined our fathers by sending them into exile, and who has blessed this remnant of your people, we praise your name. Here is your house—the house you have allowed us to build for you! May it honour you always.

"Lord, we look forward to an even greater day than this—the coming of our Messiah whom your prophet Zechariah has told us will one day rise up out of the house of David as a fountain that will cleanse us from our sin and impurity. But for today, O Lord, we offer the blood of these animals in accordance with your command to Moses." Zerubbabel nodded to Jeshua then, who went forward to the altar of the Lord and sacrificed twelve unblemished goats, one for the sins of each of the tribes of Israel.

Taken from: Ezra 1–6:18; Haggai 1:1–2:9; Zechariah 12:10–13:1.

From the Bible:

The law is only a shadow of the good things that are coming—not the realities themselves. For this reason it can never, by the same sacrifices repeated endlessly year after year, make perfect those who draw near to worship....Therefore, when Christ came into the world, he said, "Sacrifice and offering you did not desire, but a body you prepared for me; with burnt offerings and sin offerings you were not pleased. Then I said, 'Here I am—it is written about me in the scroll—I have come to do your will, O God.'"...And by that will, we have been made holy through the sacrifice of the body of Jesus Christ once for all (Hebrews 10:1,5–7,10).

Talking it over:

1. *Why was it so important for the Jews to rebuild the temple and reinstitute the sacrifices for their sins? (Because God had commanded them to make such sacrifices. See Leviticus 4. Without the shedding of blood, there could be no forgiveness of sins. See Hebrews 9:22.)*

2. *Although the remnant of Jews who returned to Jerusalem were obedient to God's command to sacrifice animals, did they rely on these sacrifices to secure God's forgiveness? On whom did they actually rely for God's forgiveness? How did they know about the coming Messiah who would purify them once and for all eternity?*

3. *Why do we not sacrifice animals to atone for our sins today?*

The Maccabees: Defenders of God's altar

Benjamin ducked behind a boulder about twenty feet from the fork in the road that led north and west out of Jerusalem. He was sure he had felt the vibration of approaching horses. No doubt these were King Antiochus' men hunting down Jews who had escaped Jerusalem over the last few gruesome months. Benjamin tucked his legs up tight, trying to disappear within a crag in the rocks. He clutched the letter he was to deliver to Mattathias, priest of the village of Modein. He had been instructed to swallow it if he were in danger of being captured.

The pounding hoofs came, thundered close, and then receded toward the north. They had not taken the road to Modein! There was still time. Benjamin crawled out and ran toward the setting sun.

Mattathias and his five grown sons had just finished dinner when they heard a knock at the door. The sons watched Mattathias nervously as he rose to answer it. These days even the most routine occurrences seemed threatening.

Mattathias found Benjamin outside, hurried him in, and took the letter. Anxiously, he sat down at the table and began to read while his sons waited.

When Mattathias finally raised his head, his face was a fierce red, and tears spilled out of his flaming eyes. "My sons…" was all he managed to say. One of them—Judas, also known as Maccabeus—gently took the note from his father's shaking hand and read aloud:

> My dear old friend Mattathias,
> I write to warn you that the unthinkable has happened since you left Jerusalem. After killing every Jew who refused to violate God's Laws in one of the many contemptible ways that our Greek "king" could devise, his men invaded and pillaged the sacred temple itself, violating even the most Holy of Holies. As their crowning dishonour to our Lord, they erected a statue of the pagan god Zeus above the temple altar, and then sacrificed a pig to this vulgar image. Of course, they chose a pig because they know that under God's Law this animal is unclean.

As you might imagine, the devout among us have fled the city in hopes of avoiding the horrible choice that Antiochus has given us: disobey our God or be slaughtered like sheep. But his men are intent on hunting us down, so the choice remains. Soon you must make it too, as Antiochus is extending his brutality into the outlying villages. Mattathias, it is only a matter of time before they arrive in Modein. Be prepared to die well, my friend.

Judas let the letter fall to the floor and grabbed both of his father's arms. "There is a way we can die well that your friend has not thought of, Father," he said, staring steadily into the older man's sorrowful eyes.

Mattathias understood, and found strength in his son's words. There was indeed a third alternative, and they would take it: they would die defending God's holy altar.

Early one morning a few days later, an official named Apelles led a detachment of the king's troops into Modein. Apelles positioned the heavily armed men around the village, and set a few to work building an altar to Zeus. They had brought along a pig.

When the altar was ready for the pagan sacrifice, the soldiers paraded the villagers into the square to watch. Because they were the priestly family of the village, Mattathias and his sons were forced to lead the procession.

When all were in place, Apelles clutched the hilt of his sword menacingly and approached Mattathias. "You are the leader here," Apelles said so that all could hear. "Be the first in Modein to carry out the king's order, as so many of your brethren in Jerusalem have done. Sacrifice this animal to Zeus and receive abundant favours from the throne." With that, he waved his free hand toward the pig standing on the new altar, inviting Mattathias to approach.

Mattathias said nothing for a long while, as he calmly fingered the sacrificial knife in his hand and glared at Apelles. The village was deathly quiet. Accepting Apelles' offer would be a clear violation of God's Law and would make a mockery of the sacrificial system that God had ordained since the time of Moses. Finally Mattathias announced: "I and my sons will follow the Lord's covenant though all others may tremble and fall before the king. We will not deviate one step from God's Law."

Preparing for the worst, the villagers hid their children's eyes. But just as Apelles drew his sword to take off Mattathias' head, an ambitious young man from the crowd stepped onto the pagan altar. "I will accept the king's favours," he said eagerly.

Relieved, Apelles and his men helped prepare the pig for slaughter. When all was ready, the young man drew his arm back to slice into the animal. At this moment of sacrilege, outrage consumed Mattathias, and he rushed forward to stab the traitor with his own sacrificial knife. Before they could subdue the pious priest and the other villagers, Apelles and his men had also perished. The pagan altar quickly followed.

Mattathias then called out to his brethren, "Whoever is zealous for God's Law and will pledge himself to maintain God's covenant with his people, follow me and my sons!" The Maccabean revolt had begun.

When the Jewish refugees hiding throughout the Judean countryside heard of the events in Modein, they rallied behind the Maccabees, choosing to die fighting for God's Law. Eventually, they succeeded in regaining the temple that Zerubbabel and his brethren had constructed 350 years before, and they reinstituted the sacrifices that the Lord had commanded them to make in atonement for their sins.

It would not be long now before Jesus, the perfect and eternal sacrifice for our sins, would come to earth and live among the Jews of Judea. The shedding of *his* blood would forever atone for the sins of those who had or would repent and believe in him.

From the Bible:

Then [Moses] took the Book of the Covenant and read it to the people. They responded, "We will do everything the Lord has said; we will obey." Moses then took the blood, sprinkled it on the people and said, "This is the blood of the covenant that the Lord has made with you in accordance with all these words" (Exodus 24:7–8).

When Christ came as high priest of the good things that are already here, he went through the greater and more perfect tabernacle that is not man-made, that is to say, not a part of this creation. He did not enter by means of the blood of goats and calves; but he entered the Most Holy Place once for all by his own blood, having obtained eternal redemption....For this reason Christ is the mediator of a new covenant, that those who are called may receive the promised eternal inheritance—now that he has died as a ransom to set them free from the sins committed under the first covenant (Hebrews 9:11–12,15).

Talking it over:

1. *Why was Mattathias so upset that the temple built by Zerubbabel was used to make sacrifices to Zeus?*

2. *Why was the sacrificial system so important to the Jews? (It was required by the Law; it was tied to their worship of God and their hope of his forgiveness of their sins.)*

3. *The Jews who lived before Christ were under the "first covenant" that is discussed in the above verses. Look again at Hebrews 9:15. Whose blood atoned for the sins of those who were under this first covenant?*

Section 4

Jesus is Prophet, Priest, King

Questions to learn:

57. What does Christ do for his people?

He does the work of a prophet, a priest and a king.

58. Why is Christ a prophet?

Because he teaches us the will of God.

59. Why is Christ a priest?

Because he died for our sins and prays to God for us.

60. Why is Christ a king?

Because he rules over us and defends us.

61. Why do you need Christ as a prophet?

Because I am ignorant.

62. Why do you need Christ as a priest?

Because I am guilty.

63. Why do you need Christ as a king?

Because I am weak and helpless.

■　■　■

Through Jesus' response to Peter's sad blunders, Peter grew to love the Lord Jesus deeply as his prophet, priest and king. Two who powerfully experienced Christ's kingship were Adoniram and Ann Judson, America's first foreign missionaries.

If Christ is for us, who can be against us?

The main road through Jerusalem was not rugged, yet Peter stumbled along it like a man who had already walked a long way through rough terrain. He and John were trying to keep pace with the detachment of soldiers that had bound Jesus before the disciples' very eyes, and were now hurrying him through the city. They could just see the soldiers' torches and spears above the heads of the Jewish festival-goers crowding the street.

Peter searched his mind for something he could hang onto—a safe thought. What he found instead were many frightening things to avoid. So much had happened in such a short time! During their Passover meal, just that evening, Jesus had washed the disciples' feet and had spoken a great deal about pouring out his blood. If that wasn't bad enough, Jesus then announced that one of the Twelve would betray him, and that they would all fall away from him on that very evening.

After that, things had happened quickly. Not wanting to fall away from their Lord as he had warned, the disciples had followed Jesus to the garden at Gethsemane—all except Judas, who had soon appeared in the garden leading several Jewish officials and the soldiers who had seized Jesus. Peter himself had pulled his sword and swung wildly at the nearest intruder, cutting off his ear. Remembering this as he staggered along the path, Peter gazed at his guilty hands. Had he really done that?

Then there was something else Jesus had said to Peter before the soldiers had come. What was it? Peter chased the memory around his mind but it would not be caught. It seemed important, but Peter simply wasn't in any shape to supervise his poor rattled brain. It would have to wait.

John and Peter soon arrived at the gate of Annas, the former high priest, into whose home Jesus had been taken. John knew him well, and convinced the guard at the door to let him inside. Peter, it was decided, would have to wait in the courtyard with the other onlookers.

The servant who opened the courtyard gate to Peter eyed him suspiciously. He was not in soldier's uniform, and she did not recognize him as one of the Jewish officials who so often came around. "Aren't you one of *his* disciples?" she asked him accusingly.

Peter cringed at the way she said "his"—with hatred and disgust. Beyond

her in the courtyard he could see men warming themselves over a fire. Some of them were probably close enough to overhear. Why should he have to answer to a servant anyway?

"I am not," he lied, and moved quickly past her to the fire.

The men already sitting around it were chatting breathlessly about the evening's events. Most of them had families at home waiting on them to celebrate the Passover, but none wanted to be left out of the excitement. No, they would all wait and see what would be done with Jesus.

"My bet is they let him go," said an older man who had been around long enough to watch plenty of blasphemers fall in and out of favour.

"Not a chance," argued the young aide of an official who was inside. "Why, he's a menace. He's got hundreds believing his lies, and…he stirs people up. One of his men tried to kill the high priest's servant this very evening!"

Had the fire not already chafed Peter's face, the others would have seen it turn red at this reference to his impetuous swordplay in the garden.

Just then, a third man noticed Peter's clothing. "Say, aren't you one of the Galileans who travels with him?" he asked.

Peter's eyes darted from one penetrating gaze to another within the tight circle of blazing faces. *"Man, I am not!"* Peter denied.

A minor official who had overheard these remarks then stepped into the circle. "Yes," he said, pointing at Peter, "didn't I see you with him earlier in the olive grove?"

Exasperated by their needling accusations, and fearful for his own life, Peter retorted in a loud voice, *"Man, I don't know what you're talking about!"* Before anyone could respond to this, however, a rooster crowed from the high priest's yard. As Peter instinctively turned toward the sound, he saw Jesus watching him sorrowfully from the courtyard of Annas' house.

The memory that Peter had been unable to grasp earlier now rushed in and claimed his whole attention. Jesus had said to him: "Peter, Peter, Satan has asked to have you. But I have prayed for you, that your faith will not fail. Before the rooster crows tonight, you will claim three times not to know me. But *when you have turned back, strengthen your brothers."*

Peter tore his eyes from his Saviour, ran from the courtyard, and wept bitterly.

Taken from: Luke 22:31–34,54–62; John 18:10–27.

From the Bible:

My dear children, I write this to you so that you will not sin. But if anybody does sin, we have one who speaks to the Father in our defence—Jesus Christ, the Righteous One. He is the atoning sacrifice for our sins, and not only for ours but also for the sins of the whole world (1 John 2:1–2).

For we do not have a high priest who is unable to sympathize with our weaknesses, but we have one who has been tempted in every way, just as we are—yet was without sin (Hebrews 4:15).

Talking it over:

1. *How was Christ a prophet in this story? (He knew beforehand what would happen, warned Peter of it, and knew what to do about it.)*

2. *How was Christ a priest in this story? (He interceded with God on Peter's behalf, then offered the sacrifice of himself.)*

3. *How does it make you feel that the Lord Jesus Christ is praying to the Father on your behalf?*

King over all kings

Adoniram Judson and James Colman bowed low to the floor and awaited the appearance of the Burman king, referred to by all as the Golden Presence. When young King Bagyidaw finally strutted into the audience hall, Adoniram stole a look. With his long black hair wound up in a turban, the Golden Presence was small but regal, wearing checkered silk pants and carrying a gold-sheathed sword.

At length, the king acknowledged the two American missionaries who knelt before him, and beckoned to the official standing by with a petition that Adoniram had written on palm leaves. The missionaries had come several days' journey upriver from Rangoon in hopes that the king's Golden Ears would hear their plea. "Very well," the king said to the official, "read."

The petition respectfully begged that the king issue an order stating that any of his Burman subjects who desired to practice the Christian religion should be allowed to do so in peace. The king pondered this for a moment, and then took his hand from the hilt of his sword and snatched the palm leaf from the cowering official. Adoniram also handed the king a carefully worded, palm leaf-sized statement of his Christian beliefs.

While the king studied the two documents, Adoniram prayed fervently for God to soften this cruel man's heart so that he would allow the gospel of Jesus to be shared openly in Burma. Adoniram remembered the day, almost seven years ago, when he and his wife Ann had arrived in this godless country as the first American missionaries abroad. He thought of her now, waiting for him at their mission in Rangoon, trying to protect the three timid but sincere Burmans who had only recently come to believe in Christ. These converts had faced threats so severe, that before he had left for the palace in Ava, two of them had asked to be baptized at night so as not to advertise their new status as Christians. All that could change, though, if King Bagyidaw would only grant his people permission to worship as God led them.

The Golden Presence read no further than Adoniram's claim that there is only one true God. At that point he looked up darkly and opened his hand, allowing the palm leaves to flutter to the floor. The interview was over, the petition denied. Adoniram and James Colman were instantly cast out of the palace.

They knew only too well what this would mean to their little mission in

Rangoon. Once word spread that the king had rejected their plea, even those few Burmans who had already come to Christ would be treated abominably—overtaxed, beaten, tortured or even killed—unless they renounced their newfound faith. No one else would come anywhere near the mission house to hear their message or receive copies of the literature that he and Ann had worked so hard to translate into Burmese so that the people could understand it. They had gambled on the king and lost. This would surely mean they would have to move the mission, perhaps out of Burma.

As they started on the voyage home, Adoniram prayed. "O Lord, at your leading we have toiled ceaselessly in this country of great tyranny to which you have sent us. And if we were able to see the end result of these efforts, as you can, I know that we would be compelled to give you the highest praise! Though I cannot now see it, please make my heart quicker to trust in the power and wisdom of my Almighty King, Christ Jesus. Please show your rule over all the world and defend your gospel in this small kingdom."

Even before Rangoon came into sight, Adoniram heard the temple bells on its many Buddhist pagodas tinkling in the wind. When they rounded the bend they saw their little group on the pier awaiting them—their wives and the three members of their mission church, Maung Nau, Maung Thahlah and Maung Byaay. It was February 18, 1820.

On Sunday Adoniram called the tiny church together and explained all that had happened in Ava before the king. "We will have to close the mission now, or you will be in great danger. You may expect persecution and suffering if you stay, but you are all welcome to come with us to our next mission," Adoniram said sadly.

Almost in unison, the three Burman believers begged the Judsons not to leave. Every danger that Adoniram described, they made light of. This from men who had so recently begged not to be baptized in the daytime so as to avoid persecution much less severe than what they could now expect!

A few nights later Maung Byaay came to the mission and asked to speak to Adoniram. "Teacher, I have been most distressed since you said you were leaving. I have found many more among my people who are examining the new religion. Some of them are close to the kingdom of God. Please stay until there are eight or ten disciples so that we can have a church that continues after you go. I know if we ask him, God will raise up one among us to become teacher of the rest."

It seemed that the dark prospect of losing the gospel of Christ altogether was having a strong effect in Rangoon. The Judsons stayed until July 19, 1820, when they determined that Ann would have to spend a few months away because of illness. Nevertheless, as their ship sailed from Rangoon, Adoniram and Ann waved to a crowd of well-wishers on shore that included ten native Burman Christians. With all their hearts, the Judsons entrusted these helpless young converts to their own mighty king, Christ Jesus, whose power prevails over the fickle opposition of earthly rulers.

And Christ proved an able defender of the faith. Today, hundreds of Burman Christians trace their spiritual roots back to the Judsons' tireless work early in the last century. Despite tremendous persecution from the current regime in Burma, they hold to their faith, looking forward to their citizenship in Christ's eternal kingdom.

From the Bible:

"You are right in saying I am a king. In fact, for this reason I was born, and for this I came into the world, to testify to the truth. Everyone on the side of truth listens to me" (John 18:37b).

Who shall separate us from the love of Christ? Shall trouble or hardship or persecution or famine or nakedness or danger or sword? ...No, in all these things we are more than conquerors through him who loved us (Romans 8:35,37).

Talking it over:

1. *Was the spread of Christ's gospel thwarted by King Bagyidaw's rejection of the missionaries' petition, as Adoniram feared it would be?*

2. *How was Christ a king to the Burman Christians?*

3. *Where does Christ rule? How does he defend his kingdom on earth today?*

Endnotes

1 Sinclair B. Ferguson, *Know Your Christian Life* (Downers Grove, IL: InterVarsity Press, 1981), 1.

2 James Reston, Jr., *Galileo: A Life* (New York: HarperCollins*Publishers*, 1994), 99 (from a letter to Belasario Vinta).

3 This triangle was used in the fourteenth century by missionary Raymond Lull. See Carl Brumback, *God in Three Persons* (Cleveland, TN: Pathway Press, 1959), 97–98.

4 John Bunyan, *Grace Abounding to the Chief of Sinners* (London: Penguin Books, 1987) (first published 1666), 16.

5 Jonathan Edwards, *Memoirs of the Rev. David Brainerd* [*The Works of President Edwards* (New York: G. & C. & H. Carvill, 1830), X, 260].

6 Paraphrased from C. Bigg, ed., *The Confessions of Saint Augustine* (London: Methuen & Co., 1899), 83.

7 Spurgeon's recollections of this sermon are quoted more fully in: Ernest W. Bacon, *Spurgeon: Heir of the Puritans*, (London: George Allen & Unwin, 1967), 23–24 (from a March 1861 sermon of Spurgeon); and Hugh T. Kerr and John M. Mulder, eds., *Famous Conversions, the Christian Experience* (Grand Rapids: Wm. B. Eerdmans Publishing Co., 1983), 129–132 (from *The Autobiography of Charles H. Spurgeon*).

Bibliography

Introduction

Soldier story

Benjamin B. Warfield, *Selected Shorter Writings of Benjamin B. Warfield—Vol. 1.* ed. John E. Meeter (Nutley, NJ: Presbyterian and Reformed Publishing Co., 1970).

Unit I

Galileo Galilei

Derek Gjertsen, *The Classics of Science: A Study of Twelve Enduring Scientific Works* (New York: Lilian Barber Press, 1984).

Morton F. Kaplon, ed. *Homage to Galileo, Papers presented at the Galileo Quadricentennial, University of Rochester, October 8 and 9, 1964* (Cambridge: M.I.T. Press, 1965).

James Reston, Jr., *Galileo: A Life* (New York: HarperCollins*Publishers*, 1994).

Bernard Gilpin

C.S. Collingwood, *Memoirs of Bernard Gilpin* (London, 1884).

William Gilpin, *The Life of Bernard Gilpin* (London, 1755).

Athanasius

Justo L. Gonzalez, *The Story of Christianity. Volume I: The Early Church to the Dawn of the Reformation* (San Francisco: Harper & Row, 1984).

S.M. Houghton, *Sketches From Church History* (Edinburgh: Banner of Truth Trust, 1980).

Kenneth Scott Latourette, *A History of Christianity. Volume I: To A.D. 1500* (Peabody, MA: Prince Press, 1997).

Dead Sea Scrolls

Thurman L. Coss, *Secrets from the Caves, A Laymen's Guide to the Dead Sea Scrolls* (New York: Abingdon Press, 1963).

Frank C. Thompson, ed. *Thompson Chain-Reference Bible* (Grand Rapids: Zondervan Bible Publishers/Indianapolis: B.B. Kirkbride Bible Co., 1983).

Geza Vermes, *The Dead Sea Scrolls, Qumran in Perspective* (Rev. ed; London: SCM Press, 1977).

John Bunyan

John Bunyan, *Grace Abounding to the Chief of Sinners* (London: Penguin Books, 1987) (First published 1666).

Unit 2

Polycarp

W. Grinton Berry, ed. *Foxe's Book of Martyrs* (Grand Rapids: Baker Book House, 1978).

Christian Frederick Cruse, trans. *The Ecclesiastical History of Eusebius Pamphilus* 4.15 (Grand Rapids: Baker Book House, 1955).

David Brainerd

Jonathan Edwards, *Memoirs of the Rev. David Brainerd*. Vol. 10 of *The Works of President Edwards* (New York: G. & C. & H. Carvill, 1830).

John Tallach, *God Made Them Great* (Edinburgh: Banner of Truth Trust, 1974).

John Wycliffe

W. Kenneth Connolly, *The Indestructible Book* (Grand Rapids: Baker Books, 1996).

Louis Brewer Hall, *Perilous Vision of John Wyclif* (Chicago: Nelson-Hall, 1983).

Bruce L. Shelley, *Church History in Plain Language* (2nd. ed.; Dallas: Word Publishing, 1982).

Williston Walker, *A History of the Christian Church* (3rd. ed.; New York: Charles Scribner's Sons, 1970).

B. Wilkinson, *The Later Middle Ages In England 1216–1485* (London: Longmans, 1969).

Augustine

C. Bigg, trans. *The Confessions of Saint Augustine* (London: Methuen and Co., 1899).

Charles Colson, *Loving God* (New York: HarperCollins Publishers, 1987).

S.M. Houghton, *Sketches from Church History* (Edinburgh: Banner of Truth Trust, 1980).

Bruce L. Shelley, *Church History in Plain Language* (2nd. ed.; Dallas: Word Publishing, 1982).

Unit 3

John Wesley

David Lyle Jeffrey, ed. *English Spirituality in the Age of Wesley* (Grand Rapids: Wm. B. Eerdmans Publishing Co., 1987).

John Pudney, *John Wesley and his World* (New York: Charles Scribner's Sons, 1978).

John Wesley, *The Journal of John Wesley*, ed. Ernest Rhys (London: J.M. Dent & Sons/New York: E.P. Dutton & Co., 1906).

Martin Luther

S.M. Houghton, *Sketches from Church History* (Edinburgh: Banner of Truth Trust, 1980).

Bruce L. Shelley, *Church History in Plain Language* (2nd. ed.; Dallas: Word Publishing, 1982).

Bard Thompson, *Humanists and Reformers. A History of the Renaissance and Reformation* (Grand Rapids: Wm. B. Eerdmans Publishing Co., 1996).

Ninety-Five Theses

Roland H. Bainton, *Here I Stand: A Life of Martin Luther* (New York: New American Library, 1950).

Henry Bettenson, ed. *Documents of the Christian Church* (2nd. ed.; London: Oxford University Press, 1963).

Bard Thompson, *Humanists and Reformers. A History of the Renaissance and Reformation* (Grand Rapids: Wm. B. Eerdmans Publishing Co., 1996).

John Newton

Heroes of the Faith—John Newton (Oak Brook, IL: Institute of Basic Life Principles, 1991).

David Lyle Jeffrey, ed. *English Spirituality in the Age of Wesley* (Grand Rapids: Wm. B. Eerdmans Publishing Co., 1987).

Hugh T. Kerr and John M. Mulder, eds. *Famous Conversions, The Christian Experience* (Grand Rapids: Wm. B. Eerdmans Publishing Co., 1983).

Bernard Martin, *John Newton, A Biography* (London: William Heinemann, 1950).

Bruce L. Shelley, *Church History in Plain Language* (2nd. ed.; Dallas: Word Publishing, 1982).

Edessa

Christian Frederick Cruse, trans. *The Ecclesiastical History of Eusebius Pamphilus* 1.13 (Grand Rapids: Baker Book House, 1955).

Unit 4

Charles Spurgeon

Ernest W. Bacon, *Spurgeon: Heir of the Puritans* (London: George Allen & Unwin, 1967).

W.Y. Fullerton, *Charles Haddon Spurgeon, A Biography* (1920 ed.; Chicago: Moody Press, 1966).

Hugh T. Kerr and John M. Mulder, eds. *Famous Conversions, The Christian Experience* (Grand Rapids: Wm. B. Eerdmans Publishing Co., 1983).

Charles Finney

Charles G. Finney, *The Memoirs of Rev. Charles G. Finney* (New York: A.S. Barnes & Co., [1876]).

Charles E. Hambrick-Stowe, *Charles G. Finney and the Spirit of American Evangelicalism* (Grand Rapids: Wm. B. Eerdmans Publishing Co., 1996).

John Williamson Nevin, "The Anxious Bench" in Keith J. Hardman, ed. *Issues in American Christianity: Primary Sources with Introductions* (Grand Rapids: Baker Books, 1993).

Mark A. Noll, *A History of Christianity in the United States and Canada* (Grand Rapids: Wm. B. Eerdmans Publishing Co., 1992).

J.I. Packer, *A Quest for Godliness, The Puritan Vision of the Christian Life* (Wheaton, IL: Crossway Books, 1990).

Maccabees

William Reuben Farmer, *Maccabees, Zealots, and Josephus: An Inquiry into Jewish Nationalism in the Greco-Roman Period* (New York: Columbia University Press, 1956).

Josephus, *Complete Works of Josephus In Ten Volumes*. Vol. 4. *Antiquities of the Jews Books X–XIII* (New York: World Syndicate Publishing Co., 1900).

Sidney Tedesche, trans. *The First Book of Maccabees* 1.20–2.27 (New York: Harper & Brothers, 1950).

Adoniram Judson

Courtney Anderson, *To the Golden Shore: The Life of Adoniram Judson* (Boston: Little, Brown and Co., 1956).

James D. Knowles, *Memoir of Mrs. Ann H. Judson* (1831 ed.; repr. New York: Garland Publishing, 1987).

About the authors

Selah Helms is a homeschooling mother of four—Andrew, Caleb, Elisabeth and Peter. From the time the children were small, she and her husband Doug, now a pastor in Crowley, Texas, instructed the family in doctrinal truth and its practical implications for the way people live.

Susan Thompson is an attorney in Austin, Texas. Her avid interest in doctrine and church history was sparked a few years ago during a leadership conference for Bible Study Fellowship.

The authors, friends since they worked together on a college magazine staff, teamed up to produce this book in a desire to delight and instruct children with the essential truths of Christian doctrine and the amazing impact it has had on people's lives through history.

About the illustrator

Caffy Whitney is a freelance illustrator who ministers out of her home studio in Kansas City, Missouri. She is also homeschooling her daughter, Laurelen. Her husband, Don, is an author, conference speaker and Professor of Spiritual Formation at Midwestern Baptist Theological Seminary in Kansas City. Don and Caffy have been catechizing Laurelen since she was two years old and regard being a part of this project as a privilege.